Debbie
How do I
Love and appre
you so much
Love
Mary Heil

Paper Dolls

Paper Dolls

Mary Hill

To my husband, Jerry—my first love. Thank you for your patience and love through all the remembering, built up tears, and joys I experienced while writing this book.

To my sweet children (Jeremy & Katie, Timothy & Irish, Jonathan, Preston, Jayne, and Rachel), for reading and re-reading my stories and reassuring me that it was okay to write them.

To my sisters, whose strength, courage, and enduring love made it possible to survive this journey.

To my mother, who inspired me from the grave. I love you, and I now understand.

A special thank you to my sweet daughter-in-law Katie, who has worked tirelessly editing, formatting, and encouraging me all the way. I am so lucky to have you in my life.

Finally, to my writing group (my amazing instructor Lisa, Deborah, Donna, Chrissy, Tara, and Bonnie), who was there from the very beginning, cheering me on and encouraging me to keep writing.

"I've learned that regardless of your relationship with your parents, you'll miss them when they're gone from your life."

-Maya Angelou

Table of Contents

Preface

I'm always amazed at how everything seems to be a life lesson; when we research one thing, it may teach us another.

I started this book as a way to put on paper the little information I could remember about my mother, who had recently passed away. I wanted to remember the stories she shared, her experiences with her mother, and why she did the things she did. What I found was a discovery of myself.

I've learned just how strong I am. Growing up, I thought it was self-preservation. But as I re-evaluate my life, I realize the experiences that are the most difficult actually make us stronger. We may learn to survive, but we also learn to be brave. Life doesn't necessarily harden us; I'm one of the softest people I know.

Life has made me compassionate and understanding. I know things aren't always crystal clear. In life we should never assume to know what another person is feeling or going through; we can only see the surface.

I once had an acquaintance tell me that I lived in a bubble. She saw me as a person who had no problems, someone who had never experienced hardships and wouldn't know how to handle them if they came. I, like most people, have my share of problems. I just never felt the need to share them with everyone. I've always left my problems at home, so she assumed I had none. She wanted me to be just as unhappy as she was, but I never saw the advantage in being sad all the time. Life is too short. It's a challenge for all of us; those who survive the challenges either go on to live productive lives or sit and feel sorry for themselves.

* * *

I want to introduce you to six women: my grandmother Auline Hastings, my mother Estelle Joseph, and my three sisters Arlene,

Lynn, and Linda. I want to share with you their lives along with my own—our challenges, our courage, our weaknesses, and our strengths.

Paper dolls—so fragile, yet so enduring. A little tape and they will last forever.

(from left to right) Me, and my three sisters, Linda, Arlene, and Lynn

CHAPTER 1

Hospital

Girls, I've donated my body to science. I have a card in my purse. In case anything happens to me, just call the number on the card."

The last thing we wanted to talk about was Mom dying. There were times when she was really mean (and sometimes we *wished* she would die), but we never meant it. No matter how cruel she was, we still loved her. When she would bring up the whole "one-of-these-days-I'm-going-to-be-gone" speech, we would completely ignore her.

Mom was forty-five years old when she decided to donate her body to science. When she died at the age of eighty-one, I thought the card had expired. Dad was cremated in 1990, and since they were still married, the Navy offered her a special military rate. We signed her up and paid for it, so we just assumed she was going that route. As it turned out, the hospital already had her donation card on file. When she passed away, hospital personnel were instructed to call the number on the card—the same card and number she told us about when we were kids.

I was holding Mom's hand when a couple of orderlies came in; they asked my husband Jerry and me to step out of the room so they could "bag and tag her." I had no idea what that meant—it all happened so fast. They explained later that it was important to preserve her body since they would be moving her to several schools of science. The procedure was different than just getting the body ready for burial.

Jerry and I stood in the hospital corridor for about fifteen minutes. When the door opened, Mom was lying on the bed inside a dark black vinyl bag. The machines that helped keep her alive were unhooked, the tubes and cords just dangling. I stood looking at the black bag on the bed, and then I turned to look at Jerry. I wasn't prepared; I hadn't said goodbye. He came to me and hugged me tightly. Then he led me out of the hospital. Jerry had to return to work and wanted to be sure I was going to be alright; I assured him I was fine. I told him I just needed to make some phone calls.

I got in my car and closed the door. Everything felt surreal, like waking from a dream and not being sure it really happened. I was sure I was having an out-of-body experience, though, because I couldn't feel anything. I made all the motions of being alive, but inside I felt empty.

I sat in my car for some time. I wanted to understand what had just happened. My mom had died, and that was it. There was no closure. We never discussed things like funerals or services. Most of her friends and family were gone. I needed to call my sisters, but instead I just sat there.

That couldn't be all there is, I thought. *After eighty-one years, this couldn't be it.*

As I sat in my car, I thought back to when I was a young girl. I wanted to go back in time, change things, and make them better. I wanted what everyone wants; I wanted good memories. Over time, what I got were bits and pieces of our lives. Good or bad, this is it.

* * *

When I was six years old, Saturday was our "clean the house" day. Since we knew all the words by heart, we would listen to Mitch Miller's "Sing Along with Mitch" records and do just that. ("It's Only a Paper Moon" was my favorite.) We cleaned every Saturday, all day long. If Mom was in the mood, she would tell us stories from her childhood.

I remember how she talked about her parents. Mom would get really serious because she wanted us to understand that life was hard. Grandma and Grandpa were both deaf-mutes. As children, they both contracted spinal meningitis, and the high fever caused them each to lose their hearing. They met as young adults at a community dance for the deaf; soon after, they fell in love and got married. Mom said they were really happy.

Mom explained that Grandpa adapted well to being deaf. He worked a regular job as a machinist; he had a lot of friends and several hobbies. One of his hobbies was making beer in their basement, and he'd have Mom help him because the corks would pop when the beer was ready. (Mom would help by listening for the pop.) They spent quality time together because she was his first-born and his little girl.

After Grandma's second child was born, Grandma started getting sick. She became unsure of herself and seldom left the house. If anyone came to the door, Grandma would send Mom to talk to them. She became more of a recluse as time went on.

When Mom was eight years old, the nuns from the local Catholic church paid a visit. As Mom interpreted for her parents, the nuns explained they were worried that Mom was using sign language exclusively and not speaking with her voice. They took her to live in the convent for a few weeks.

I asked Mom once what it was like to live in a convent. She said, "I hated it. The nuns were mean. If I used my hands to talk, they would tie them behind my back or hit them with a ruler."

But at the end of three weeks, Mom was talking without sign language, so they let her go home.

When Mom returned, Grandma's condition was worse. She had turned mean. She seemed to blame Mom for everything, thinking her daughter had abandoned her.

Grandma usually waited until they were alone (like when Mom was in the bathtub), and then she would come in and beat her with a wet washcloth. Mom said those beatings were the worst because they would leave big welts on her back and legs, and sometimes they would bleed. She said Grandma would collapse afterwards and cry like a baby. Mom ended up consoling Grandma for the pain Grandma inflicted on her. The younger would hold the elder, rocking her like a baby.

My heart always ached for both of them. It was obvious to me, as Mom told me these stories about Grandma, that Grandma was sick. As a kid, Mom kept telling herself that she must have done something to make Grandma mad. *It must be my fault*, Mom would think.

Grandma's condition continued to deteriorate. Fifteen years passed, and finally, one night, the authorities came and took Grandma away. When Mom told me this story, my heart broke for them all over again—for all the pain they had suffered. Mom had cried as she recounted that night.

* * *

The year was 1943. My mother was twenty-four years old and still lived at home, taking care of Grandma. She had just fallen asleep when her father woke her, and the look on his face told her something was terribly wrong.

He signed for her to get dressed. The state authorities were there to take her mother away because the neighbors couldn't take it any longer. They lived in a brownstone apartment building in Brooklyn, New York, and the walls between them and the neighbors were very thin. My grandmother had been sick for years, and she often screamed in her sleep. The neighbors were good people, but enough was enough.

Mom knew this day would come. Still, she was unprepared when she entered the living room and saw six strange men, four in white jumpsuits and two in plain clothes.

Things seemed out of control. Grandma was screaming and running around in her blue flannel nightgown, with her dull, gray hair (usually pulled back in a bun) lying long and stringy around her shoulders. Her eyes were bulging and red-rimmed from constant crying. Her skin, once flawless, was now dry and ashen from lack of care. She looked scared.

The two men in plain clothes did all the talking and note taking, while the other four wrestled her down. Two men held her as the others fastened her into a straightjacket.

Her screams were like nothing you can imagine. Mom explained that the hearing impaired have no idea what they sound like; when Grandma screamed, it sounded more like a screech—loud and shrill. She kept screaming and crying as the authorities sedated her, which forced her to calm down. They directed all conversation to Mom, the only other hearing person in the room. The men explained that they were taking Grandma to a state mental hospital for evaluation. They gave Mom all the necessary information and directions, and they told her to wait a week before going to the hospital.

It took only two of them to lift Grandma's small, limp body, strap her to a gurney, and carry her out to the panel truck that would take her to the hospital. Mom and Grandpa walked out to the porch with them, and the orderlies put Grandma in the back of the truck. Two of them rode in the back with her, the other two rode in the front, and the men in business suits left separately.

Mom and Grandpa stood on the porch and watched as they drove away. They were each deep in thought and didn't know what to say. Mom had a feeling Grandma would not be coming home again.

Mom remembered the good times before Grandma got sick. In the beginning, she still had moments when she was her old self. She would smile, put her arms around Mom, and tell her she loved her. But those moments happened less and less; Mom couldn't remember the last time Grandma actually acknowledged her. She didn't seem to know anyone in the family anymore, and Mom was glad her three brothers weren't around. They had joined the military as soon as they could, just to escape the nightmares at home.

For the past few years, Mom had tried to talk to Grandma. She signed to ask her if she wanted eggs for breakfast, or something to drink, but she got no response. Mom had set up regular schedules to feed her and take her to the bathroom. She'd tried to get her to take baths or brush her teeth, but Grandma had fought her all the way, crying and fussing or flat out refusing to cooperate.

One time in particular, Mom ran a bath for her, put her favorite bath salts in the tub, and then went to get her. Grandma was sitting in her usual chair, so Mom reached for her hand and led her to the bathroom. Grandma took one look at the water in the tub, started to scream, turned around in a panic, and ran into the wall, knocking Mom to the floor. Mom just sat there stunned.

Mom knew Grandma needed professional help, but how could she put her own mother away? It was hard to acknowledge her relief when the state officials came to take Grandma to the hospital. As the panel truck drove away, Mom prayed that Grandma would finally get the help she needed.

Mom and Grandpa waited out the week and then visited the hospital. The floors were tiled and the walls were painted a pale green. A plaque on the wall read "Pilgrim Hospital was built in 1930. It was designed to house 12,500 patients on one hundred acres of land, and it holds the record for being the largest hospital in the world."

They were met by a sour-faced nurse sitting behind a beige metal desk. She handed them a clipboard and instructed, "Only your name and the person you are here to see."

No pleasantries, only the facts. Then she indicated with her eyes that they should take a seat.

Their names were called, and they were escorted to a visitors' lounge. It was a large room with a black leather couch and several chairs scattered around. A nurse entered, wearing a calf-length white uniform and a stiff white hat. She told them that Grandma's prognosis was unknown, so an expert would be coming in to evaluate her. She then led them into another wing of the hospital, explaining that they'd moved Grandma because her screaming was disturbing the other patients. Also, during several sudden outbursts throughout the week, the nurses had to physically restrain her.

They entered her tiny room that had only a bed, a nightstand, and a metal hospital table. Mom said Grandma looked small lying in her bed. Her hair was sticking straight up, her eyes were sunken in her head, and she looked much older than her forty-six years. She wore a hospital gown that had once been white but was now a dull gray. It hung loosely on her frail frame.

She didn't even stir when they approached the bed. Grandma's mind was definitely somewhere else. She had that distant look in her eyes; Mom always wondered where Grandma went when she had that look.

They tried to talk to her, and Mom even held her hand, but Grandma didn't respond to her touch. She was heavily medicated, and they stayed only a short time.

The doctor's results were due in the next couple of weeks. Until then, they would go home and wait.

* * *

Deaf-mutes do not mince words. When they talk, they say exactly what they mean. So, on the ride home from the hospital that day, Grandpa turned to Mom and told her that he was in love with a woman named Josie. They had been having an affair for years. He told her he was moving on with his life and that she should do the same. Her mother was sick and would not be returning home, and the family needed to accept that fact.

Mom was in shock. Part of her wanted to be angry with him; she wanted to blame Grandpa for Grandma's illness, but she knew that wasn't fair. Grandma was sick, and it wasn't anyone's fault. She realized that she needed to face it and move on with her life. This was not going to be easy, however, because taking care of Grandma had *been* her life. She would need to do something different.

Mom waited another two weeks or so before returning to the hospital. When she arrived, she was greeted by Dr. Anderson, the resident doctor assigned to Grandma. He asked where her father was, explaining that he really needed to talk to Grandpa as well.

Mom explained that her father had distanced himself from the situation and, by default, she'd been appointed as the decision-maker. Dr. Anderson escorted her to his office.

As they entered, the first thing he said was, "Are you aware your mother is four months pregnant?"

Mom backed up and slid into the only other chair in the room. Her legs were suddenly weak, and she was completely taken off guard.

"No, I had no idea," she stammered.

Dr. Anderson went on to say they were concerned because they had kept her medicated since she arrived. They were going to stop all medications and try to keep her comfortable until the baby was born.

He then asked, "Do you have anyone who can take care of the baby?"

She couldn't think. "I don't know," she answered. She would have to give it some thought.

He proceeded to tell her that it would take time to evaluate her mother's mental condition. He had no answers for her right then. Next, he led her to Grandma's room, where Mom anxiously approached the bed and signed, "Hello."

Grandma stared straight ahead and then started to scream. She became more and more agitated, her eyes bulging and her face turning red and distorted.

They backed out of the room. The doctor told Mom not to take it personally; Grandma just needed time. He urged her to stay away for a while, to give them a chance to work with her. He told her to make arrangements for the baby and share those plans with him. She agreed and left the hospital.

Mom had no idea Grandma was pregnant. What a shock that information was. There was only one person Mom could think of with the means to care for a new baby: Aunt Gertie.

* * *

Aunt Gertie, Grandma's older sister, owned and operated a hotel in New York City. Mom remembered when she lived and worked for Aunt Gertie at the hotel. It was 1929, and Mom was ten years old.

Aunt Gertie's hotel was a real hot spot in New York City. Celebrities like Abbott and Costello were regular guests; so many important people stayed there. Aunt Gertie was considered wealthy, and she helped a lot of family members over the years.

Times were tough—the Great Depression had hit. People were walking blindly up and down Broadway looking for work. Food was scarce. Aunt Gertie was fortunate because her hotel was still doing well. But Mom was too young to understand how desperate people were because of the economy. Some people lost everything and took their own lives; crime was at its highest because people couldn't even feed their families.

One day Mom noticed a lot of commotion outside. People seemed to be scurrying around. Aunt Gertie warned her and her younger brother, Charlie, to stay inside the hotel, but when Aunt Gertie was busy, she and Charlie ventured out for just a minute. The first thing she saw was people gathering around a man handing out tickets.

"Here little girl, here's your ticket," he said. She took it and put it in her pocket.

Charlie always knew what was what. "Let's sit over here," he said, and they climbed onto a large keg next to an alley around the corner from the hotel.

There was a man on a big stage talking loudly, but it was hard to hear what he was saying over the noise of the crowd. It was all so exciting.

Suddenly, someone said, "Hey, look at your ticket, it could be a winner!"

A winner? Mom thought. She took the ticket out of her pocket.

The man grabbed it and yelled, "Here it is! She's the winner!"

Before she knew what was happening, she was being escorted to the stage. A basket of food, so large she couldn't carry it, was thrust at her. Her brother Charlie ran to get his wagon while she stood in the middle of the stage in shock.

Charlie said that when he returned, Mom was still standing in the same spot. She was in a daze, frozen in the middle of the stage with her finger in her nose.

Charlie never let her forget it. Forty years later, he was still telling that story.

Aunt Gertie was appalled when they returned with the large basket, embarrassed that people might think they were poor and needed the food.

* * *

Mom went directly from the hospital to see Aunt Gertie, who still owned the hotel and was doing well for herself. Mom informed Aunt Gertie about what was happening with Grandma. She explained there was no one to take care of the baby, and then she asked her aunt if she would consider raising it. She also told Aunt Gertie there was a chance Grandma would not be coming home again. Aunt Gertie always yearned for a child of her own, and she was genuinely excited. She started making arrangements immediately. She would be at the hospital when the baby was born.

Grandma was in labor for almost an entire day, but the doctor said everything went well. They would let her body heal and then work on fixing her mind. They still hadn't given her a diagnosis. She was definitely sick, but she hadn't received the final review and the pregnancy had complicated everything. The doctor and nurses weren't sure if Grandma even realized she had given birth. But Bobby was born and Aunt Gertie took him home. He was a cute little guy.

Mom stayed away from the hospital, just as Dr. Anderson had asked.

* * *

Grandma had been in Pilgrim State Mental Hospital for almost a year, and Mom was trying to sort things out. Should she pack Grandma's things or leave them where they were? She kept holding onto the hope that one day her mother would come home.

While Mom was sitting in Grandma's bedroom, Grandpa came in with a guest. "This is Josie," he signed.

Mom didn't know how to react; this was the woman Grandpa told her about, the woman he'd been seeing and had fallen in love with. Mom politely said hello, and the women shook hands. Josie seemed like a nice person, and it was obvious the couple was in love. But Mom had such mixed feelings. She wanted Grandpa to be happy, but she didn't want to be disloyal to Grandma. She needed time. It was hard to accept that Grandpa was moving on with his life. *How could he do that so easily?*

After Grandpa returned from taking Josie home, Mom asked, "How are you going to tell the boys?"

She knew this would be a difficult question to answer. After all, sons are supposed to protect their mother, and she guessed they would not take the information lightly.

Grandpa just shrugged his shoulders and signed, "They already know."

"They know?" she signed, agitated. "What do you mean they know?"

He looked so calm as he signed, "I introduced them to her over a year ago."

Mom wondered, *Was I the last to know?* She signed furiously, "Who else knows about Josie?"

"Relax," he calmly signed. "You weren't ready to meet her. You were too busy taking care of your mother, and I thought it was best to keep it from you. Don't be mad at your brothers; I asked them to keep my secret."

She was stunned. *How could they all know and not tell me? What about Mom? Do we just throw her away and forget her? What if she gets better? What do we tell her?*

Mom panicked. She had so many questions, but she knew they couldn't be answered right then. She would just have to wait and see what happened.

* * *

Grandma lived at Pilgrim State Hospital from 1943 until 1976. In 1975, Mom went back to New York to visit Grandma. It had been thirty-one years since they had last seen each other. Mom approached Grandma's bed and saw that she was coherent; she didn't have that far off look in her eyes like the last time Mom saw her. It seemed as though she was better, and maybe Grandma would remember her this time.

She signed, "Mom, it's me, your daughter Estelle."

"I don't have a daughter," her mother responded.

Mom kept insisting that she *did* have a daughter. Mom said, "It's me, Estelle, don't you remember?"

Grandma looked at her and signed, "You're too old, I can't have a daughter that old."

Mom was fifty-six, and of course she looked different. She continued to try and convince Grandma that she was, in fact, her daughter. Mom brought up stories from when they lived together.

She told her about how, at eight years old, she had been sent to live in a convent until she started talking with her voice instead of her hands.

Something was familiar about that story. The look on Grandma's face seemed to show recognition: *Could this really be my daughter?*

Mom was getting frustrated, and the time to leave was drawing near. She signed that she was going to leave and, with tears in her eyes, Mom turned to go. Something told Grandma that if she let her leave she would regret it; something deep inside said that this was her daughter. All of a sudden, Grandma pounded her fist on the side table. Mom turned and saw her mother crying, and Grandma signed that she knew she was her daughter.

They both began to cry. Mom ran to her bedside, and they embraced, holding each other tightly. Mom took her coat off and sat down in the chair near her bed. They had so much to say, so much to catch up on. They talked for hours. Mom filled Grandma in on as much as she knew about the rest of the family. Mom told her about her own children (Grandma's four granddaughters), who all lived in California. Mom confessed that life had been hard at times, but she never stopped thinking of her.

When it was finally time to leave, Mom knew this would probably be the last time they would see each other. Grandma told Mom she loved her and was sorry for the heartache she knew she'd caused.

Mom cried all the way back to her hotel. She cried for the loss of her mother—for all the years she missed not having her in her life. Grandma died a few months later.

Grandma suffered from depression. Back in 1943, they called it "melancholy," an illness that can be mostly cured with a little pill today. The cure in 1943, however, was to turn the lock and throw away the key.

Mom got closure, yes. She was grateful for the insight and opportunity she had to visit her mother a short time before her death. But she was left with regrets. Grandma missed out on thirty-one years of birthdays, Christmas mornings, ballgames, Thanksgiving dinners, growing grandchildren, graduations, weddings, heartaches, and happy times.

Estelle, 7 (right), with her mother and brothers

Top: Aulene Wittman with daughter, Estelle
Bottom: Estelle, age 5

Top: Aulene Hastings Wittman (my grandmother)
Bottom: My grandpa and his girlfriend Josie

CHAPTER 2

New York

In 1944, New York City was hopping. Young men and women were auditioning for parts in all the Broadway plays as singers, dancers, and actors. The competition was tight. Mom always wanted to sing on stage; she had a good voice, and all she needed was the chance to prove it to the world. Now that she was free from taking care of Grandma, she would get a job and start auditioning. Most work was scarce—people took whatever was available.

Nightclubs were opening everywhere, so some worked as hatcheck girls, and some sold cigarettes. Mom thought she was one of the lucky ones as she went from table to table, taking pictures. Photos with the stars, photos with your gal, group photos. It was mostly fun; still, eight hours on her feet with a heavy camera around her neck reminded her it was a job. Some nights she didn't even get a break. Mom worked on commission, so every picture sold was money in her pocket.

It had been a long night, and she was exhausted. All she could think about was getting home, taking off her shoes, and going to bed. She wished she had taxi money, but she was still struggling and couldn't even consider that luxury. She had to walk several blocks just to catch the bus, and took comfort in knowing it was only a fifteen-minute ride home.

She was so deep in thought as she walked to the bus stop that she didn't even hear them approach. Before she could react, someone grabbed her from behind. Her hair was pulled back so hard she thought she would die from the pain of it. Everything happened so fast, and everything was loud as she struggled to understand what was happening. It was too dark, and all she could see were shadows.

All at once, the commotion stopped. She heard someone running toward her. She didn't know whether to scream or cry, so she just sat there. She was still not certain what was happening.

An unfamiliar but gentle voice asked, "Are you all right?"

She squinted to focus on the silhouette of a man in front of her. "I'm fine," she said, and then paused. "What happened?" she asked.

He explained that he was leaving work when he saw two suspicious looking men approach her from behind. He could tell something was going to happen, so he followed them from a distance to make sure she was safe. When they attacked, he stepped in. He said he probably broke the nose on one guy and got a few kicks into the other.

Her vision finally adjusted to the dark, and she could see that he had kind eyes. She felt safe—even though she was shaking—and thanked him as he helped her to her feet. His hands felt warm on hers, and that feeling of safety grew as she held them. As he walked her to the bus stop, she learned his name was Pete and realized she was falling in love.

* * *

Pete and Mom dated for several months. After the night of the attack, Pete began waiting outside the nightclub and they'd walk to the bus stop together. He was her shining knight. He had saved her life, and she felt a gratitude she couldn't explain.

Their love was mutual and they got married. Soon they were expecting a baby. They were excited and everything felt right between them. There was only one small problem. Pete was of Asian descent; although it wasn't a problem for them as a couple, her family did not approve. As much as she loved her family, she also knew they were prejudiced and would not accept an interracial marriage. Fearing her brothers would be cruel, she avoided introducing them to Pete.

Pete and Estelle lived in a city apartment several blocks from her family. To avoid seeing them, they would walk around the block. Mom knew sooner or later they would have to deal with them, but she wasn't sure when it would be. Her brothers solved that dilemma when they surprised her at the club one night. They hung around until closing, making their meeting with Pete inevitable.

Pete was waiting for her when they emerged from the club. She introduced them to her new husband. The tension was high and her brothers were hostile.

Her brother Benny was fast to recoil, stating flatly, "I'm not going to have a Chink in the family." He went on to say that she had disgraced them all. Benny asked, "How could you do this to us?"

All she could do was try to explain the situation; they were in love, happy, and expecting a baby.

Jackie, the oldest, got really angry. He said he would never accept a "Chink" baby, and that if Mom didn't get rid of both of them, she wasn't welcome in his home.

It was horrible, and she cried all night. Pete held her and soothed her; after all, it was 1945, and he was used to this kind of treatment. But she wasn't. He tried to console her, saying that her brothers would get over their prejudice toward him and the baby in time. She just needed to be patient.

Months passed. The baby was coming soon, and she hadn't heard a word from her brothers. She and Pete found themselves walking where her family would not see them. They started to argue. She missed her family and felt lonely without them. She knew in her heart that her family was wrong, but she couldn't help missing them and found herself snapping at Pete more and more. He didn't deserve it; he was so patient and kind.

* * *

It was 1950, and Mom was divorced and raising a child alone—not exactly the life she had pictured for herself. It just got too hard. Pete felt like they were always hiding. Their happy home became filled with bitter arguments. Pete tried to be patient, so it wasn't his fault; she was the one who pushed him away. She just pushed and pushed until he had nowhere to go.

Aunt Gertie gave Mom a job at her hotel and a place to raise her six-year-old daughter, Arlene. Mom was very grateful. With the divorce behind her, and now that she was getting back on her feet, Mom returned to her dreams of singing. She had a great voice, and she desperately wanted to sing. Now all she needed was a break, so she continued to audition.

Mom was leaving an audition when she met him. He was tall and very handsome.

His name was Michael. He was in the Navy, and there was something very alluring and mysterious about him. She was hooked from the start. When it came to love, Mom never thought things out; instead, she just dove in, heart first.

Michael was a bachelor who made it very clear that he loved his freedom. She told herself she could make him fall in love—that all she needed was time. They continued to date, and when he went out to sea for six months, she wrote him daily. But he was too busy and tired to write her back.

When he came home, she was standing at the dock to meet him. Looking back, she realized that she had been smothering him, that he needed his space. He even said so many times, but she kept right on until he just stopped getting off the ship. He stopped coming around, and he didn't return her letters or messages. She was finally realizing that it was over between them when she missed her period. It was obvious Michael did not want to see her. But she convinced herself that if he knew about her pregnancy, he would realize he really *did* love her, and they would live happily ever after. She contacted the chaplain on his ship, and the procedure was simple. The Navy made their men do the right thing. They were married late in 1951, and their daughter Lenore was born in April, 1952. Mom was really happy. Michael was miserable.

Top: Estelle with brothers
Bottom: Arlene and Santa at New York Macy's

Estelle and Michael's Wedding party (1951)

My dad (front center), Michael Joseph

CHAPTER 3

Guardian Angels

I was born in Brooklyn, New York. My given name is Marianne Joseph. Mom was going through one of her Catholic phases. (Get it? "Mary and Joseph.") I never liked my name. In school they would either call me "Joseph Marianne" and assume I was a boy, or mispronounce the "Marianne." Eventually I shortened it to Mary.

We stayed in Brooklyn for another year before Dad was transferred to California; while we were living in Long Beach, he went overseas off and on for a couple of years. I don't remember anything about our stay in California, since I was only a toddler. It was not until forty years later that my mother unloaded her painful secrets.

* * *

Flash forward to 1995. My mom was seventy-six years old. She came over on a Saturday, and I was in my office catching up on work. She looked like she had something on her mind; her mouth puckered and she squinted her eyes when something was wrong.

"What's up?" I asked, as she sat down across from me. She thought for a moment and then said, "I have something to tell you—it's been on my mind for years. I've kept a secret I don't want to keep anymore."

"What kind of a secret?" I asked, shuffling the papers on my desk.

There are some things you just don't want to keep to yourself or take to your grave. Mom had a secret that was eating her alive. She needed to tell someone, and I was that someone.

She took a deep breath, and the words just flowed from her mouth. "Between the time you were born and the time your sister Linda was born, I gave birth to two other children, a boy and a girl."

She waited to see what I was going to say. I thought I was prepared for anything she had to say, but honestly, I was not prepared for this.

"What do you mean you had two other children!? Where are they?" I know I sounded as shocked as I felt.

As if she didn't hear my questions, she went on to say, "There were two separate pregnancies, two different fathers, and neither one was your dad."

Mom explained that she was lonely since Dad was often stationed either overseas or somewhere far from home. It was no secret that their marriage was not one of love, but rather of convenience. Whenever Dad went away, Mom would look for companionship, comfort, or simply a man to pay attention to her. Mom was raised Catholic and did not believe in using birth control.

My brother and sister would be in their forties by now, I thought. My mother offered very few details. All she really knew or remembered was that the boy was born first. She went to a Catholic hospital, gave a false name, and never even saw him. The nuns took him away the minute he was born. The girl was born about a year later at home with the assistance of a friend. Mom said she had been afraid. My dad was due home soon and she didn't know what to do.

In an act of desperation, she fed her new baby girl, dressed her in warm clothing, and wrapped her in a blanket. She then took the baby and placed her under the front steps of a mobile home. Mom knew that a family lived there and hoped they would take her in, but she didn't hang around to find out. She walked away and never looked back.

"I was scared and desperate," she said.

"What hospital!? What mobile home park!?" I almost screamed.

I couldn't believe I was hearing this, and I could see she wasn't going to tell me anything else. She had a way of shutting down.

"I don't remember anything. Please don't ask me anything else," she pleaded. Once she told me the basics, all she wanted to do was forget. She had freed herself of the burden by handing it over to me.

I was so frustrated. "You have to tell me more. You have to think. Who was there? Where were you living at the time?"

She just shrugged her shoulders and said, "I'm sorry, but that's it. I can't remember."

I had a younger brother and sister out there somewhere, I thought. Was it possible I could have passed them on the street?

"Mom, you have to try and remember!"

Over the next couple of years, I called several adoption agencies and asked them what information I would need to locate my siblings. They said I would need dates, places and names. I guess I knew that, but I was hoping they would tell me something miraculous. I wanted the impossible—to give them a photo of myself, have them run it through the computer and come up with my real brother and sister.

On random occasions, I would ask my mother again if she could remember anything else. Once she said she thought the boy had been adopted by a celebrity, either a politician or someone in the entertainment world.

Mom is gone now, and I still don't know what happened to my brother and sister. I wonder if I'll ever know.

* * *

After California, we moved to Chattanooga, Tennessee, where my youngest sister Linda was born in 1957. Mom got a job working as a waitress in a restaurant close by, and I met Rose.

Mom worked full time, so she hired a lady that stayed with us all day. Rose cooked our meals and took very good care of us. She would rock me and tell me stories. I loved her, and she loved me. I was five years old.

We didn't know it at first, but Rose didn't know how to read. Mom would leave notes for Rose all over the house, telling her different things she needed to do. I remember Mom getting really irritated because they weren't getting done.

Then it dawned on her, and she asked, "Rose, do you know how to read?"

Tearfully, Rose said, "I do not."

From that day on, Mom began teaching her to read and changed her methods of communication. She would plan the lunch menu by leaving out specific cans of soup so that Rose would know to prepare chicken noodle and tomato. She would put the clothes that needed ironing with the ironing board, and so it went. Rose became part of the family. I loved when she arrived in the morning, and I cried when she left at night. I knew Rose had a husband waiting for her at home, but I loved her so much that I didn't want her to leave.

We lived in a Navy community in Tennessee. All the kids on the block had dads in the Navy, so we all played together. It was a fun time. Then a new family moved into the neighborhood. They were a large family with six kids. The boys were mean and loud and the girls weren't much better, just not as loud.

One day Rose came outside and told us to come in for lunch.

"Okay, Rose, we're coming," we said.

The new kids looked shocked and asked why we were listening to "the black woman." They called her names I didn't know. I had never heard the things they were saying, and I was really confused.

"But I love Rose," I said, in tears. I remember how they laughed at me and said more ugly things.

I went home for lunch really upset. When Rose saw I was crying, she picked me up and sat with me in the rocking chair. She soothed me the way she always did. I cuddled with her, and when I had settled down, she asked me what was wrong and why I was crying. I was so confused; I looked up at her and very seriously said, "Rose, I love you, but I hate your black face."

I thought she would comfort me some more and tell me everything was all right, but instead she slowly put me down and didn't say another word.

When Dad came home, Rose announced she was quitting. Later that day, Dad told Mom that Rose had quit and he didn't know why. Mom questioned us, and I told her what the neighbor kids had said and what happened between Rose and me. I told Mom what I had said to Rose, and Mom knew right then what to do.

Mom and Dad loaded us in the car, and we went to find Rose. Mom talked to me all the way to Rose's house. She explained about prejudiced people and how hurtful and mean they could be. Mom never taught us to be prejudiced. We never knew there were different races. Sure, we were young, but the truth is that Mom never taught us to hate.

Rose lived across town. It took forever to get there, but we finally found where she lived. I remember vividly that the streets were very muddy, not paved and in bad repair. The house she lived in was like a shack with four unpainted walls. There were several of these cabins in a row, and everything seemed so dark. There were only a few streetlights. I remember a really big, shiny car in the driveway. (Mom said Rose's husband owned a Cadillac.) Dad parked the car and agreed to wait with my sisters while Mom and I went in.

We knocked, and Rose answered the door. Inside, the house was very neat and clean. The furniture was old but in good condition, and everything looked like Rose. She loved doilies, and they were everywhere, on the tables and even on the backs of the chairs and couch. We sat down, and Mom told Rose she heard about what happened and how sorry she was. She told her how much I loved her, how confused I was about what the neighbor kids had said, and she begged Rose to please come back. We all cried and hugged each other.

Rose returned the next day and stayed with us for the next two years. We weren't allowed to play with those kids anymore. They moved soon after and are probably doing hard time somewhere.

* * *

My oldest sister Arlene had been living with my mom's Aunt Gertie since she was seven. When she was twelve years old, she came to live with us again, after we'd moved to Chattanooga, Tennessee. I never knew why she didn't live with us before, but it was nice having her live with us again.

Life was comfortable. Dad was working a lot and seemed to be behaving himself; he wasn't drinking as much, which in turn meant he was staying out of trouble. Dad had always been stationed on a ship, but now he was working in a small recruiting office in Chattanooga. I think maybe he got into some trouble on the ship and they moved him. He was always getting into trouble because of his drinking and gambling.

Arlene loved living in Tennessee. She had a lot of friends and did really well. During that time we liked to go to the drive-in movies a lot; it was cheap, and we could all go for the price of a carload instead of per person. The people who owned the drive-in tried to make it entertaining by having contests and games to keep the kids busy.

One time they had a watermelon eating contest, and the winner won a Davey Crocket jacket. This Davey Crocket jacket was fancy—it was brown suede with fringe on the arms and across the top, and had "Davey Crocket" written across the back. Arlene got it into her head that she really wanted it; she said she honestly never wanted anything as bad as she wanted that jacket. So she entered the contest.

There were quite a few kids that entered; they had tables and tables lined up with watermelons. The judge said, "Ready, set, and go!" and they started eating. You had to eat it all, and then they gave you another slice. It was like watching buzz saws buzz through each one. Slice after slice—what a mess. There were watermelon rinds and juice everywhere. Some kids ate so much they actually threw up, and others threw up when they saw someone else getting sick. In the end, Arlene won the contest. She was so exhausted and sick to her stomach that she didn't even enjoy the jacket until the next day. She has never liked watermelon since, and even the sight and smell make her sick.

But she loved her jacket, and she wore it everywhere. One afternoon, she was standing on the porch just daydreaming. She had her jacket lying across her shoulders, with the arms of the jacket flapping on the side. She took the sleeves and wrapped them around herself, just playing around. She must have stood on the porch for a while before going back in the house.

Later that afternoon, she called her girlfriend to see if she could come over. Earlier that day, the girl's mother had driven by and seen Arlene hugging a boy on her porch. Her mother said it was inappropriate behavior for a nice girl, so they couldn't hang out anymore.

Arlene was shocked. "But it wasn't a boy! It was just me in my new Davey Crocket jacket!"

She tried to explain, but it sounded so ridiculous that she just gave up.

Many years later, she asked, "How do you defend yourself over a jacket?"

* * *

Shortly after my birth, Mom took me to a Catholic priest to have me blessed. She had all four of her daughters blessed, but there was only one difference between my blessings and those of my sisters: The priest told my mother I was special because I had a guardian angel. I don't know why he told Mom that I had a guardian angel, but I held on to that all throughout my childhood. I can compare it to a lucky penny—give a kid a penny, tell him it's lucky, and he will believe it. The comfort my guardian angel gave me was priceless, and I wish Mom had given this gift to my sisters. Believing you are not alone through harrowing times gives you hope, and I can't imagine not having that.

I believe in fate. What I mean by fate is that things happen for a reason. We may not know what that reason is right away, but I guarantee that we will come to realize it at some point in time.

In 1958, Mom was still working as a waitress at a local diner. Rose took good care of us, but on days when she was sick or not available, my father would watch us if he was home. On one occasion, he took us to eat at a different diner than Mom's, and I just thought that he didn't want to bother her at work.

When my mom got home, we were coloring. I had just figured out how to color inside the lines when she asked us what we did that day. Innocently, I looked up from my coloring book and said, "Daddy kissed a waitress."

I never dreamed this would cause such a problem. All of a sudden my mother got really angry. She asked me again, "What did you see?"

I repeated, "Daddy kissed a waitress."

Mom pulled me up from the ground by my arm and took me into the living room to face my dad. Dad was sitting in a chair reading the newspaper, when she turned to me and told me to repeat what I'd said. By now I knew something was terribly wrong. But I said for the third time, "Daddy kissed a waitress."

The look on Dad's face went quickly from shock to anger. He turned to me and said, "You're lying!"

I don't remember this part very well, but Mom said that I stood tall, placed my hands on my hips, and yelled, "You did too! I saw you!"

With this, my father got angry and slapped me hard across the face.

Things changed after that. I became my mother's favorite, her loyal snitch. My sisters loved me but resented me at the same time because of my mother's favoritism. My father ignored me from that day forward. I didn't understand at first why he was so angry with me, and my feelings were hurt.

But this is where "fate" comes in. It turns out that my father was a very sick man. He had been molesting my two older sisters for years before my mother found out. But I was spared; he knew I would reveal his secret, so he left me alone. My reputation for telling my mother everything saved my life. I know, without a doubt, that my life would have gone differently if I hadn't seen Dad kiss that waitress.

Do you believe in guardian angels?

CHAPTER 4

Back to California

It was 1958 when we left Tennessee for California, and I was five years old. When we arrived we moved into a Quonset hut—a "prefabricated structure made of corrugated steel." They were used as barracks, latrines, offices, family housing, and bakeries, among other things. (It was not the nicest place we ever lived.) Mom said it was old, drafty, not very pretty, and that she hated living there. The Navy furnished it with cold, black leather furniture. We lived there for a couple of years until we were approved for some new Navy housing.

I was not ready to go to kindergarten, but Arlene took me anyway. I was scared and didn't want to be there. I didn't know anyone since we had just moved. All the Navy kids that lived in the huts went to the same school, which was just down the block. When Arlene dropped me off, she didn't stay to see that I was okay because she had to get to school herself. She simply showed me where to go, and then she left.

Once she directed me, I walked towards the classroom but never went in; I just kept on walking until I got home. Dad was home at the time, and he was surprised to see me. I must have looked pathetic. I was crying so hard my nose was running. He took some pity on me but then said that I had to go back to school, and he walked me back. I waited several minutes and again returned home. Dad walked me back again, and this time he talked to the teacher so she would make sure I stayed.

I finally got the hang of it and didn't fuss about going to school. Lynn and I would wait for Arlene, and then the three of us would walk home together. The Quonset huts were set on dirt, so it was hard to keep the house clean and even harder to keep ourselves clean. We played outside during the summer when everything was hot, dry, and dirty and during the winter when everything was cold, wet, and muddy. I was a tomboy; Mom said she could never buy me anything white, since I ruined everything I wore. I either tore the knees out of my pants or ripped buttons off my tops, and my shoes were always scuffed and dirty.

* * *

Do you remember, as a child, wanting something someone else had? Wanting it so badly it made you crazy with envy?

When I was five, the object of desire was a pair of clear plastic princess slippers, decorated with a thousand diamonds on top. The minute a girl slipped them on her feet, she felt like a princess. One girl in the neighborhood owned a pair, and my sister and I couldn't believe how beautiful they were. What we wouldn't do to own those slippers! My older sister, Lenore (who we called Lynn) was six years old, and she wanted those slippers more than anything. But they might as well have cost a million dollars; she knew Mom couldn't afford to buy them. They were a luxury, and money was tight.

Knowing Lynn loved those slippers made the owner of them a little snot. She wore them whenever she came over and refused to let Lynn try them on. She would parade in front of us, showing off like a model, moving her foot from side to side. One thing led to another, and Lynn couldn't stand it another minute. When the girl took the slippers off, Lynn grabbed them and ran out of the house. She ran a few blocks to a drainage ditch and threw them in. The hole was deep, and we could see the shoes glittering, but we couldn't reach them. The girl ran home crying. We just stood there looking down at those beautiful slippers; we couldn't believe Lynn had thrown them in the ditch, and we knew she was in big trouble.

It felt like an eternity before Mom came home. The girl's mother caught up with ours before she went in the house. We were doomed.

Mom finally came in and immediately called for Lynn to "Come here right now!"

Lynn walked in with pure fear on her face. Mom didn't say anything, but with a look that could kill, she handed Lynn a department store bag and told her to open it. Lynn slowly opened the bag and brought out a brand new pair of plastic princess slippers. Mom knew Lynn wanted those slippers, so she went on her lunch break to buy her a pair; they were going to be a surprise. Shock and shame showed on Lynn's face.

Mom was so angry that she grabbed the package from Lynn and proceeded to hit her over and over again with the slippers. When the beating was over, my mother very calmly told Lynn to apologize and give the new slippers to the girl next door. I remember standing there crying for Lynn and hating my mom. My sister had suffered enough without the physical abuse. Lynn slowly got up from the ground, her head held high. She walked next door, apologized, and gave the neighbor girl the new pair of slippers.

We never talked about it. Years later, as I was reminiscing about the past, I asked Lynn if she remembered the princess slippers. She said she didn't remember the incident at all.

* * *

Mom didn't take many snapshots of us when we were kids. But we do have one picture Mom paid for when a professional photographer came around selling packages to all the Navy families. Arlene was in her early teens and she looked so grown up. Lynn and I wore pastel dresses that Mom had made. Linda was the cutest one-year-old you ever saw; she had big dimples and held a stuffed animal (one of the many props the photographer gave us).

We lived in the Quonset huts for a couple of years until we were approved for some new Navy housing. Mom was excited because this was a brand new housing development, and we were finally going to live in a nice house. Our new house had never been lived in by anyone but us. It had new carpet, new appliances in the kitchen, three bedrooms, two bathrooms, and a nice large living room with a sliding glass door that led to a big backyard. We even had a garage, although we didn't have a car.

Mom immediately made friends with the people next door. John and Delores had two boys and a girl named Marsha. Mom was the happiest I had ever seen her.

Navy housing had very strict rules. Once a month an official would come and inspect our house; this was called "the white glove test." He checked everything to make sure we were taking good care of their property. He even inspected the yard to make sure the grass was being cut and trimmed. Dad was out to sea. That left Mom and four girls to take care of everything.

We were young—Arlene was now fourteen, Lynn was seven, I was six, and Linda was two—and it was hard work. We used the military lawn mower and other equipment that was stored in a garage about a half-mile away. My older sisters and I would walk there, check out the equipment, carry it back to the house, mow and trim the yard, and then walk back to return it since we could only keep it for the day. It was exhausting, but we did it.

One Monday morning we all left for school, which was across the street from our house. This meant we could walk to school, come home for lunch, and walk back.

Mid-morning, there was a knock on the door. A neighbor told Mom that our puppy had gotten out of the yard. He tried to follow the kids to school and was hit by a truck. Mom panicked. We had only lived in our new Navy housing for six months. It took so long to get accepted. She was scared that if the Navy found out it was our puppy in the street, we would get written up, kicked out, and have to go back to the old, cold Quonset huts.

Pure terror took over. All she could think about was getting it cleaned up. I had just walked in for lunch. Mom grabbed a broom and dustpan and ordered in that angry "don't question me" tone, "Clean it up!"

In shock, I walked to the street and cleaned up the mess.

Was the Navy really so strict that it would blame her for a dead puppy in the road?

I was only seven years old. I couldn't go back to school that day. I cried for the loss of my puppy and the devastation of cleaning the remains off the street.

* * *

1963 was the year of my tenth birthday. Mom was taking me to the musical *Paint Your Wagon*, starring Frankie Lane, at the Old Globe Theatre. This was a rare experience for me and a real treat for Mom, who loved musicals. A friend had given her the tickets, and she really wanted this night to be special.

We arrived with plenty of time to spare. Mom and I went to the refreshment counter to get a treat, and she told me to pick anything I wanted. Talk about a tough decision!

We rarely had treats because they were expensive. And with three siblings at home, what we did get we had to share. This time I got to pick something just for me. I looked in the glass case and saw large boxes of Good and Plenty, Red Hots, Junior Mints, Milk Duds and Hershey bars. There were also sodas, popcorn, and bonbons. This was harder than I thought. I didn't want to regret my choice. I loved them all, but in the end I chose Milk Duds. The lady handed me the largest box of Milk Duds I'd ever seen; it was theater-sized, and I could hardly believe it was all mine. I held onto it tightly.

We got a program and found our seats. The theater was so large that I felt small, like an ant at a picnic. The curtain came up, and the stage came alive. I don't remember the story or the faces of the actors. It was honestly like a dream. The costumes were bright, the music loud. I just remember seeing Mom so happy. She loved music and was in her element. Mom had a tough life, with a lot of heartache and tears. It made me happy to think that maybe, for one evening, she could smile and forget life was so hard.

Most of my good memories happened in 1963. I loved Chesterton Elementary School and spent many afternoons and weekends in the playground. Mom could see it from our kitchen window, so we were allowed to play there as often as we wanted.

My teacher was patriotic and talked a lot about how lucky we were to have fathers serving our country and keeping us safe. I had a better understanding of why my dad was gone so much, and I actually felt proud of him. I remember standing and saying the pledge of allegiance. Kids who goofed off or didn't say it were sent outside, but I loved saying it. I stood tall and said it as loud as I could.

I remember getting my first real sunburn that year. I was out playing, and I looked down at my arm. I had a huge water blister where the sunburn had been. I screamed and ran home. I thought I had some dreaded disease, but Mom just popped the blister and sent me back out to play.

Christmas was the most memorable. Our Christmases before this one had not been happy events. Mom seemed so sad, and money was always an issue. Mom was always reminding us about what little money we had, but this year was different because she actually asked what we wanted. I didn't even have to think about it. I knew immediately that I would give anything for a Kenner "Give a Show" projector. It was like having my very own cartoon. The toy projector was powered by a battery, with a small light bulb that projected the image onto the wall. Several cartoon strips were included. My favorite one was "Casper the Friendly Ghost." There was no sound, just the cartoon, but it was great. I couldn't believe my luck that Christmas. It was so much fun; I invited all the neighborhood kids to watch cartoons at our house.

I can't pinpoint what happened that year to make it so good. I honestly think that Mom being happy about the new house and the extra money probably made all the difference.

* * *

Maybe part of the reason we were so happy that year was because Dad was gone for months at a time. But when his ship came back to port, Mom would get us all dressed up and take us down to the docks. We'd go early in the morning while it was still dark, and we would wait for hours. Once the ship docked, it still took several more hours for Dad to come to shore. Sometimes we were gone all day. While we waited, we watched as other sailors got off the ship and greeted their loved ones. Because things were so much cheaper in Japan, most of the men brought back presents for everyone; they had China dinnerware and crystal glassware for their wives, Samurai swords for the boys, and geisha dolls in beautiful wooden boxes for the girls. We sat patiently, waiting for our dad to get off the ship. Mom assured us, "Your dad probably brought you all something special."

We were so excited we could hardly sit still. When Dad finally came down the stairs, we noticed that he wasn't holding anything but a small box. We thought he left everything on the ship; he probably had so much that it would be hard for him to carry it all. When he got closer, he smiled like he was really happy to see us. He took Linda from Mom, hugged her close, and handed her the box he was carrying. Mom asked him what was in the box, and he said he brought something special for his baby girl. He never mentioned what he had for the rest of us and we never asked. We eventually realized that he didn't bring anything else. Even the little stuffed dog he gave to Linda had probably been purchased from the store on the ship because it wasn't anything special. He never said another word about it. I always wondered if he felt bad about that when most of the men brought gifts home to their families after every trip.

Years later, after meeting his ship so many times, Mom stopped bringing us to the docks. I was relieved; I hated the whole ordeal because it was always cold, dark, and disappointing. I overheard Mom telling our neighbor that Dad had girlfriends in every port.

When he went to Japan, he had a girl waiting for him. No wonder he never brought us anything; we weren't even a thought to him. Each time Dad came home, he and Mom would start fighting, and then he would return to live on the ship again.

* * *

It was third grade and I was nine years old. I shared a desk with a girl named Kathy. Kathy was boy crazy; she liked all the boys in our class and at recess she always hung out with them.

That year we had a new boy named George move into the neighborhood. He was different from the other boys in class. They all had fathers in the navy, so they had traditional Navy haircuts, just like their dads. George's dad had been stationed in England. He had long hair and an English accent. He was so cute. Of course, Kathy put dibs on him; she thought he was mysterious and hung around with him every day. I didn't tell anyone, but I liked George, too. I thought he was different and he was nice to talk to.

One day George brought invitations for the whole class to come to his ninth birthday party that was two weeks away. I was excited. I took the invitation home and told Mom I really wanted to go, and that I wanted to get him something nice for his birthday. Mom said we didn't have the money, so I couldn't go. I was devastated; if I didn't go, then Kathy would have him all to herself. But she liked everyone—it just wasn't fair. I never liked anyone until now. I had to go to his party. What could I do?

I went into my room looking for anything that would pass as a birthday present. All my stuff was old and girly—a ceramic dog with a chip on his foot, stuffed animals, and hand me downs from my older sister Arlene. I had a plastic swan that used to hold a tube of Arlene's lipstick that she threw in the trash and I took out; I couldn't believe she could throw something that beautiful away. I figured if I loved it so much, then George would love it, too.

I showed Mom what I decided to give George for his birthday, and then I begged her to let me go. Mom took one look at it.

"It's a swan and it's pink," she protested. "Are you sure this boy is going to like it?"

I told her I was sure. It was one of my favorite treasures, so of course he'd like it. With that, Mom agreed to let me go to the party. She bought a Candy Pez dispenser and we put it in the swan. Mom thought if George didn't like the swan, then at least he would like the candy.

I told everyone, including George, that I was going to his party. George was really nice; he smiled like he was glad I'd be there.

When Saturday came I got all dressed up. I wore my best outfit. Arlene walked me to George's house, and we planned for her to pick me up in a couple of hours.

Everyone was there when I arrived. His house was Navy housing like mine, the same style as our house only turned around. The garage door was open, and they had picnic tables lined up for everyone to sit at. Kathy of course, was sitting next to George eating hot dogs and drinking punch. I didn't know who to talk to or what to do. George saw me walk up and moved over so I could sit on the other side of him. I was nervous and excited as I handed him his gift. He looked so handsome in his navy blue blazer.

We were sitting side by side. The cutest kid in class was sitting right by me, and I was in heaven. Then the strangest thing happened: Kathy asked George a question. Just as he turned his head to answer her, I looked up for a second and noticed that he had dirty ears. I was stunned. *How could that be? How could this cute boy not clean his ears? What about his parents? Didn't they notice his ears?*

My mom made us clean our ears every day. She said no matter what, you always keep yourself clean. All of a sudden I didn't want to sit by George. I was shocked and disgusted. George for me would never be the same.

For the rest of the year every time I saw him all I could think was, *Why did I give him my swan?*

* * *

After Linda was old enough to go to kindergarten, Mom got a job working as a bookkeeper for an accountant named Barbara Hutchinson. I remember the name because I liked the way it sounded: "Hutch-in-son." It kind of rolls off the tongue, and "Joseph" was just so plain, with no pizzazz. That year, Mom enrolled us in the after-school program at Chesterton Elementary School. Linda was five and in kindergarten; I was nine and in fourth grade; and Lynn was ten and in fifth grade. We went right after school. They gave us a snack, we did our homework, and we got to play with toys that we'd never played with before. I remember they had tiddlywinks and pick-up sticks.

I remember the pick-up sticks in particular, since one time a boy was playing and a stick flew right into his eye. He screamed, they took him to the nurse, and his parents came and took him to the doctor. He came back to school a couple days later with a patch on his eye. For some reason I told everyone that he lost his eye, but he didn't—he just had to wear a patch for a couple weeks. It reminded me of when Mom used to say things like, "Don't do that, you could poke your eye out!" I thought maybe Mom really knew what she was talking about.

Mom said that the ladies in charge of the after-school program told her that we were too well behaved. They thought we needed to loosen up—they said we were too quiet and never did anything without asking permission. Mom was strict about our behavior; she drilled us constantly on how to answer an adult and when to say "please" and "thank you." She used to say, "If I ever hear you talk back to your teacher, or another adult, you will really be in for it when you get home." I never really knew what "in for it" meant, only that it had to be bad. And I wasn't taking any chances.

I think about it now and realize we were in constant fear of getting in trouble. If we had to go to the bathroom, we would hold it for as long as we could, just so we didn't bother anyone. When they gave us snacks, we were afraid to eat them for fear we would get in trouble. I realize now that our thinking was not right. Mom wasn't even around, and we were afraid of her. She was good at mental warfare.

* * *

One of my fondest memories of this time involved my collection of paper dolls. They were just perforated cutouts of boys and girls that came with outfits to mix and match; the paper clothes had tabs to help secure them to the paper figures. Some girls I knew used bobby pins to hold them on. I never owned a real doll, so when mom subscribed to *McCall's* magazine and we learned there was a different Betsy McCall paper doll each month, we thought we had died and gone to heaven.

These paper dolls became our treasures. My sisters and I kept them in a shoebox because we knew they were precious, and we were devastated if even one of the tabs broke off. Just looking at them brought me pure joy, and I would lose myself imagining the new clothes were my own and I was the doll. My favorite outfit was a red jumper with white polka dots, red shoes, and a sunbonnet that matched the jumper.

Marsha lived next door. She was my sister Lynn's age, a year older than me. Her parents and ours were drinking buddies. We spent a lot of time with Marsha, who also had paper dolls. She was the only girl in her family, and we had four in ours, so she loved coming over to our house and spending the night when all of our parents went out.

Unfortunately, we shared a lot more than paper dolls with Marsha. There were nights when our parents would bring the drinking back to our house after the bars closed. Their voices were loud, and we would sometimes huddle together in one bedroom, fearing the wrath we knew would come. We hadn't done anything wrong, but we knew we would suffer the consequences if they decided to wake us, which was usually by yelling for us. If we didn't respond fast enough, they would come into our room and practically drag us out, hitting us along the way. They would wake us in the middle of the night to clean or prepare food for them, and yell and hit us some more if we didn't do that fast enough. People who drink usually become happy or mean. If they are happy, they get really happy, but if they are mean, they are really mean. For some reason I only remember the mean.

We ran into Marsha later in our adult years. She was struggling with life. She was drinking heavily and making poor choices with men. Sometimes the cycle gets broken, and sometimes it keeps evolving. Life is like my paper dolls—very fragile. If we are not careful, a tab can break off, and we are never exactly the same again.

* * *

In 1963, The Beatles made their debut on the Ed Sullivan show, and the youth of America went wild.

In 1964, *A Hard Day's Night* came out in theaters, and I was not yet eleven years old. RC Cola was introducing its soft drink by offering a special promotion: admission to see *A Hard Day's Night* for only six RC Cola bottle caps. We didn't have money to go to the movies. Most people would just run out and buy a six-pack of RC Cola, but we didn't have that kind of money either. I remembered seeing a man fling his bottle cap on the ground outside the local market one day as he took a swig of his RC Cola. I thought there must be thousands of them on the ground, so I got permission from Mom for Lynn, our friend Marsha, and me to walk through the neighborhood looking for bottle caps. Mom said that if we found enough bottle caps for all three of us, we could go.

We scoured the neighborhood. We searched outside the local markets and the shopping center. Every time we found one, it was like finding gold. When we found the last bottle cap we needed, all three of us screamed, jumped up and down, and hugged each other. We were going to see The Beatles!

The Saturday matinee was at 2:00pm. We walked to the movie theater since we only lived a few blocks away. The line was so long it circled around the building, but we didn't care. We were going to see The Beatles' first movie. Mom let us watch them on "The Ed Sullivan Show" and we were star-struck.

We sat in the back of the theater, in the last row on the right side. The anticipation was so thick we could barely breathe. Marsha brought money so we could buy candy, and I had a Chick-O-Stick (like a Butterfinger without the chocolate). I was so excited to see The Beatles that I threw up and never ate another one again.

As the lights went out, it became completely silent. I honestly think we all held our breath. I was so worked up I thought my heart might burst. When The Beatles appeared on the screen, they were magical, and all we could do was scream, cry, and scream again. I was only ten and maybe not completely sure what I was feeling, but I remember that every one of us was crying. We weren't just crying; we were hysterical—we kept taking big gulps of air and struggling to breathe. Some girls worked themselves up so hard that they actually passed out, and ushers appeared to carry them out of the theater.

The screaming was uncontrollable. I cried and screamed so much I actually lost my voice. George was my favorite Beatle. Everyone liked Paul, but I never liked what everyone else liked, so I liked George. All the Beatles were mysterious. They had those beautiful British accents and long hair. They were perfect; I went from paper dolls to The Beatles overnight.

* * *

I'll never forget what he looked like. His name was Bill.

I was ten years old and in the fourth grade. I only remember that because it was the year I won an autograph book for writing the best scary story at school. I took it everywhere I went; I was proud of it and wanted everyone I saw to sign it.

One Saturday afternoon, we were visiting friends for a barbeque. All the kids were in the backyard playing with the rabbits when we got there. (Mom's friends raised rabbits and had several cages.) I ran to the backyard to show the kids my autograph book. When I turned the corner of the house, I ran smack into the most beautiful man I'd ever seen. He must have been eighteen years old and he was in a Navy uniform that made him look older and even more handsome. After I slammed right into him, he helped me up, and for the rest of the day I became his shadow. Bill was on the same ship as Mom's friend's husband, and he had invited Bill to the barbeque.

Poor Bill—I followed him everywhere. I listened to every word he said and I couldn't take my eyes off him. I was smitten. I heard the adults comment and smile about my obvious attachment to him, but I didn't care. He was so sweet. I'm sure he could have used a break from me, but he didn't complain; he just looked at me and smiled.

After the barbeque we all watched some television. I sat as close to Bill as I could. I was in heaven. When Mom said it was time to leave, I was crushed. Mom's friend saw my dilemma, but she also knew that Bill was leaving the next morning to go out to sea and that he probably would not come back to San Diego. She told me, and my heart broke. I started to cry. I had never felt that kind of heartache before, and I couldn't be consoled.

Mom suggested I have Bill sign my autograph book. I remember he felt so bad; he knew I had a crush on him, but he didn't know what to do or say. Graciously, he signed my book. He wrote: "Thank you for a nice day. Bill." We left, and I cried all the way home. I slept with my autograph book that night, thinking I would treasure it forever.

* * *

In 1964, Dad came home from Japan. It was always difficult when he came home. I'm sure it was the same for most military families. Mom was in charge while Dad was gone, and then Dad came home and wanted to be in charge. My parents argued about that and everything else. I remember one Saturday in particular; I had no idea I was opening a can of worms when I repeated what we learned in catechism that morning. Mom was at the kitchen sink washing potatoes for dinner, and Dad was milking a hangover with a cup of coffee and his newspaper at the kitchen table.

"Sister Katherine asked us to go home and ask our parents what came first, the chicken or the egg."

I was thinking on the walk home that it had to be the egg and innocently said, "Heck, you can't get the chicken without the egg."

Mom said she thought it was the egg too. Dad instantly got mad. "It's the chicken, Goddammit! Those nuns don't know a damn thing."

Mom went nuts. "You don't know anything! Try going to church for once in your life, and then we can talk about it."

Instantly they were both furious. Mom said, "Girls, go to your room."

And there we stayed.

We heard shouting; they argued the rest of the day and into the night. We were hungry and wanted to go into the kitchen, but we were too scared because we had learned long ago that it took nothing for their anger to turn from each other to us. We would just hide out. We finally fell asleep. I vowed to never listen to Sister Katherine again. And who the heck cares what came first?

When we woke the next morning, I was surprised the house was so quiet. Dad was gone, and Mom was still asleep.

I went into the kitchen. The potatoes were still in the sink. I realized we never had lunch or dinner. Mom and Dad fought all night over something as ridiculous as "the chicken or the egg."

Dad didn't come home for several days. I wished he would never come home again. They always fought about everything, but "the chicken or the egg" topped the chart.

They just wanted an excuse to fight. Dad was an atheist. What difference did it make to him what came first? If Mom chose chicken, he would have argued for the egg. They hated each other and took every opportunity to show it.

* * *

My parents had very little in common. Their main interest and social activity was to meet with fellow drinkers at the local American Legion Hall and drink all day. Arlene was sixteen and usually babysat; when she couldn't, waiting for our parents from sun up to sun down became our Saturday schedule. Lynn was only eight, I was seven, and Linda was three. We sat in the parking lot of the local American Legion in a 1955 Chevy.

We were prisoners. We had strict rules. There was no whining, crying or complaining, but we were allowed to talk quietly. If we were good, and if they remembered, we got a Coke and some chips to share. There were many times they forgot. Sometimes we just sat there for up to twelve hours. We didn't know any different; we didn't know to complain or who to complain to, anyway, so we just sat.

Then at the end of the night, after drinking all day, my father would get behind the wheel of that 1955 Chevy and drive us home.

Estelle in front of a Quonset hut

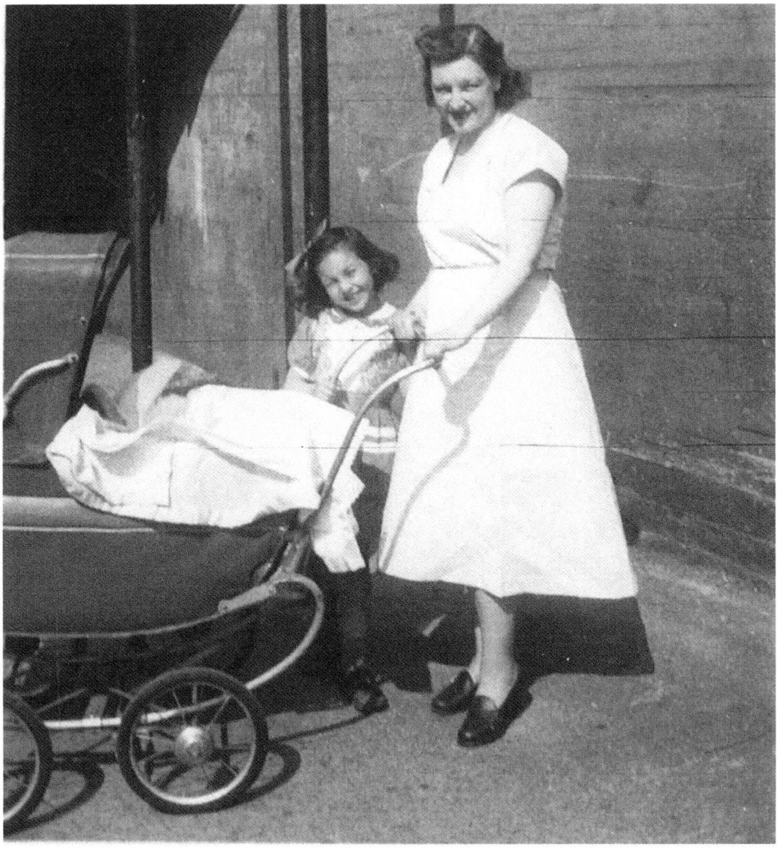

Top: Arlene and Estelle (with Lynn in a carriage)
Bottom: Me and Lynn dressed up on Easter Sunday

Top: Christmas card with (from left to right) Arlene, me, and Lynn
Bottom: Me and Lynn

(from left to right) Me, 6; Mom; Lynn,7; Arlene, 14.

(from left to right) Me, 4; Arlene, 12; Lynn, 5. Mumps.

Top: (from left to right) Lynn, 8; Arlene, 15; me, 7. Halloween.
Bottom: Me and Lynn in front of a Quonset hut

CHAPTER 5

Sign of the Times

I was in the fifth grade, and we were called in from recess. Our teacher was Mrs. Chapman, who was always so upbeat and energetic. But when we returned to our classroom that day, we knew immediately that something horrible had happened. Mrs. Chapman was talking to another teacher at the door, and they were both crying. We knew something was up, so we were all on our best behavior. We sat quietly while she tried to compose herself. It took a couple of minutes, but very slowly and very seriously she announced, "President John F. Kennedy is dead."

She went on to say that he was shot and then taken to the hospital, where he died shortly thereafter.

We all just sat there. Mrs. Chapman started to cry again, and I immediately started to cry. I didn't cry because President Kennedy was shot and killed, but because Mrs. Chapman was crying. I always cried when someone I cared about was crying. We were fifth graders; we couldn't understand the impact this particular news would have on our lives.

Our teacher had a radio in the classroom, and we heard our local news anchor announce, "John F. Kennedy, our thirty-sixth President of the United States, was hit in the head and throat when three shots were fired as the presidential motorcade was traveling through the main business area of Dallas, Texas."

"The presidential party," he went on, "was driving from Dallas airport to the city center when witnesses said shots were fired from the window of a building overlooking the road. The president collapsed into Jackie Kennedy's arms, who was heard to cry, 'Oh no.' Seconds later, Governor Connally was also hit. President Kennedy's limousine was driven at top speed to Parklands Hospital immediately after the shooting. The president was alive when he was admitted but died thirty-five minutes after being shot. He died on November 22, 1963, at 1:00 pm."

I went home that day and asked Mom why someone killed President Kennedy. She didn't answer me—just stared at the television set. She was engrossed in the news; it was on every station. We got only three stations: 6, 8 and 10. For several weeks all everyone aired was news of John F. Kennedy, his life, his family, and his presidency. I remember my little sister Linda whining because she couldn't watch cartoons.

Mom was in one of her moods, and this sad news only added to her depression. Mom stayed in bed all day glued to the television. I was still confused and found myself next to Mom, watching and trying to understand. The news told us how wonderful he was and all the good he had done. How could anyone kill someone like that?

Until that day I hadn't given much thought to the news or what was happening in politics, but I became intrigued. John F. Kennedy was definitely a loved man. He was our youngest president, and I, like most females in those days, thought he was the most handsome president we ever had. He had a charisma about him that drew us in. He was a war hero. His family's name was world-renowned. His wife and children were shown on the news, and it broke our hearts to see their strength. John F. Kennedy, Jr. was only six years old as he stood in front of his father's casket, and with the dignity of a grown man, saluted his father. You could have heard a pin drop. The sight was heartbreaking and patriotic.

The assassination of our president was an event in history that stayed with you; anyone alive during that time still remembers where they were when it happened.

* * *

Growing up in a house full of girls can be tough because girls can be the meanest. They gang up on each other, keep secrets, and are very sneaky. It's hard to have a group of girls that do not have problems. It's okay to have two girlfriends, but add another girl in the mix and you are asking for trouble.

One particular Saturday, we decided to make a tent. I have to admit it was a great tent, probably one of the best I'd ever seen. We made it outside between two trees in a large yard between our apartments. There were about five of us hanging out that day. We brought things from our homes to make it a really cool tent. I brought my favorite pillow, and others brought blankets, china sets, dolls, and stuffed animals that we used as chairs. As the day wore on, the tent just got better and better. Pretty soon, other kids from the neighborhood wanted to play in our tent. But we had worked so hard on it that we got possessive, and our meanness came out; we didn't want to share it with anyone else. We told the other kids to make their own tent, and then we shut the flap of our very cool tent as if we were closing the door on them. This made them mad, and one thing led to another.

Lynn, three of our friends, and I were having our afternoon tea. We had a teapot full of water and crackers someone had brought from home. One of the kids we didn't let play in our tent ran home to his older brother to tell on us. His brother was a really mean kid who was going to teach us a lesson. He picked up the biggest rock he could find—it looked like a boulder to us—and threw it right in the middle of the tent. It landed on the top of my sister Lynn's head and busted it right open. She screamed, her head started to bleed and it was horrible. We all started to scream. Lynn began running, and by the time she got home blood was everywhere. It was running down her face, and her clothes were covered in it. Mom took one look at her and panicked, but the Avon lady was at our house, and she helped to calm Mom down. When it's not your child, it's easier to think straight. The Avon lady assessed the damage and saw that the cut was quite deep. She drove Mom and Lynn to the hospital, where Lynn got ten stitches.

We were all pretty upset. Lynn went straight to bed, and Mom went over to the bigger kid's home to talk to his parents. Our tent was dismantled, and everyone took their stuff home. I was really sad. It was the nicest tent I'd ever seen. Mom said we were all really lucky. What that boy did was dangerous, and someone could have gotten killed. I still think about that Saturday and how we could have done things differently; we could have let the other kids join our group and share our tent. It was such a pretty day.

* * *

This incident made Mom realize that she needed to get her driver's license. She was forty-two years old and a mother of four, and she needed to be able to drive in case of an emergency. What she found out later was that being able to drive gave her a freedom she had never had. She became more self-assured and self-reliant. She no longer had to ask people to give her a ride or leave any of us behind; instead, she just loaded us all in the car, and that was that.

When she first learned how to drive, it was behind-the-wheel training with a driving instructor. She received her license very quickly, but didn't have much experience or confidence in her ability to drive. I remember we would be somewhere, and when we got ready to leave, she wouldn't know how to turn the car around in the direction she needed to go. So she would knock on a stranger's door and ask him or her to please turn her car around for her. It's amazing how many nice people there are in the world. They would look a little confused when she first asked, but realizing she was dead serious, they would shrug and turn the car around.

We were constantly getting lost. She never got excited or nervous about being lost; she would just try and make an adventure of it.

She continued to get lost during almost every trip she went on. She said there were always kind people who would point her in the right direction and that we should stop worrying about her.

Some of her older grandchildren experienced her "adventures." She always made them fun; they never knew until afterwards that they were actually lost.

Right after Mom learned to drive, I got a severe ear infection, and I was in constant pain. I hardly ever got sick or complained to Mom about not feeling well, so when I screamed out in pain because my ear hurt so badly, she took me seriously. She loaded all of us in the car late at night and drove like a mad woman to get me to the Navy hospital, cussing like crazy at anyone that got in her way. Even though I was hurting, I thought, "Wow, Mom really cares about me." In reality, I should have been thinking, "This woman is dangerous behind the wheel, and we will be lucky if we make it to the hospital in one piece." She admitted later that she was really scared.

After Mom got her license, she became the family's designated driver, which was perfect since my father drank all the time. Once while she was driving them around, they got into a fight. My father threatened to burn my mom with a cigarette. She pulled over to the side of the road and told him to get out of the car. They screamed at each other some more, and then my dad opened the door to get out. But before he was safely out of the car, Mom put her foot on the gas and took off. He was knocked out of the car and hit the ground. She was so mad she didn't even look back, so she had no idea he had broken his arm. Dad ended up calling a taxi and going to the Navy hospital. He came home late that night with a cast on his arm. So much for Mom being the designated driver when Dad was around; it gave her way too much power.

* * *

We lived in San Diego, only minutes away from Tijuana, Mexico. Mom decided she wanted to see Tijuana, so she loaded us into her car and headed for the border.

We didn't know to be afraid. We visited several large Catholic churches because Mom loved all the ornate fixtures and stained glass. Wearing our old doilies on our heads, we emerged from one church to find Mom's car being towed away by the Tijuana Police. Apparently, Mom hadn't seen the "Taxi Only" sign she parked in front of.

Mom yelled at the police, "Take that off my car, right now!" The police officer had no idea what she was saying as he continued to hook up the tow bar. Mom was five feet, two inches tall, and everyone I knew was afraid of her. She had a way of demanding attention, and this was no exception.

When the police officer refused to budge, Mom loaded us in the car and refused to get out. Nothing the police officer said or did could coax her out of the car.

It seemed Mom had met her match. The police officer towed our car with all of us sitting in the back seat.

We arrived at the police station in the morning. Mom argued nonstop with her broken Spanish. By late afternoon, we were hungry and exhausted.

A stranger came in and saw our pathetic situation. We had been sitting on the dirty floor of the police station all day, just wondering if we would ever get to go home.

After a few minutes, we found out that the fine was only $2.00 for parking in front of a "Taxi Only" sign. Mom paid the $2.00 fine, and we went home.

* * *

In 1964, Dad didn't come home much; he was gambling, and money was tight. I didn't know people could come to your house and take your stuff. The first time this happened was sometime between fourth or fifth grade. Two men came to the door; they handed Mom some papers, she read them while they waited, and then she let them come into the house and take our living room furniture. They took our couch, chairs, end tables, and coffee table. I watched in wonder as they loaded the pieces in their truck and drove away. After they left, Mom went into her bedroom and cried. I asked my older sister Arlene why those men took our furniture. We had just gotten it when we moved into the house. She said that Dad didn't pay for the furniture so they took it back.

Then, a few months later, another man came and took Mom's sewing machine. We knew Mom was really mad this time because she yelled at the man, tore up the paper, and threw it on the ground. She really loved that machine. She made all our school and church clothes with it. She asked the man, "What am I supposed to do now?" He ignored her, loaded the sewing machine in his car and drove away.

Finally, a man came and took Mom's kitchen knives. She called them her cutlery set. This time Mom cried, and then she laughed.

I overheard Mom asking our neighbor, Dolores, "Who gets their cutlery repossessed?"

"Repossessed." I looked it up in the dictionary. It meant, "taken back when payment is not made." Mom told Dolores that Dad was a gambler. He played poker with the guys on the ship or he went to the racetrack. He liked betting on the horses and dogs, and he lost a lot of money that way.

Dad felt that since Arlene had gotten married and moved out, Mom would need less and less money every month. But we eventually had to move to low-income housing. This meant we could no longer live in our nice new house. We moved to an old apartment complex. This was still Navy housing, but it was very old and very ugly. The apartments were more like two-story townhouses. The kitchen, dining room, and living room were downstairs, and we had two bedrooms and a bathroom upstairs. Mom had one bedroom, and we shared the other.

We moved about five miles from our nice house, and we had to change schools. I didn't care where we lived as long as Mom was happy, but Mom was unhappy, and, in turn, we were all unhappy. She was drinking more, and her moods were unpredictable. She would come home when the bars closed, wake us up, and pick any reason to be mad at us. Either we didn't clean the house to her satisfaction or dinner wasn't waiting for her. We tried to please her, but she was never satisfied. I remember one time Mom had left a note to take chicken out of the freezer and cook it for dinner. Lynn was fourteen years old and in the ninth grade, so she was in charge while Mom was out. Lynn had tons of homework and decided against the chicken, so we just made sandwiches.

When Mom came home after the bars closed, she was expecting chicken waiting for her. She was furious. She took the frozen chicken out of the freezer and began hitting Lynn over the head with it while she slept. Lynn screamed. Mom kept hitting her until she finally got up and went into the kitchen.

Mom made Lynn thaw and cook the chicken. Lynn's head was bleeding, but Mom was too mad to care. Lynn got a napkin and, crying silently, wiped the blood from her face.

Mom always said, "Stop that crying or I'll give you something to cry about." So we learned not to cry out loud no matter how much it hurt.

While all this was going on, Linda and I just stayed in bed and pretended we were sleeping. If Mom knew we were awake, she would hit us, too. Lynn wasn't mad at us for faking; she would have done the same thing. I think she was glad Mom punished only her this time. We always tried to stick together since we were all we had.

Lynn made Mom's supper and then went to bed. The following day, Mom stayed in bed all day. Lynn went to school even though she had a bad headache; she would rather sit through her classes in pain than stay at home with Mom.

Mom always felt deep remorse the day after one of her fits of rage. She never apologized, but she would sometimes stay in bed for days in a deep depression.

While we were living in the old apartment complex, Mom developed a craving for Spanish peanuts; she sent us to the store to get them for her almost daily. She would lie on the couch and eat them while she watched TV. Eventually she weighed over two hundred pounds, which increased her depression. She always wore an old housedress, a size twenty-seven and a half, and we tried to cheer her up by putting our money together to buy her a new one. She never fixed herself up or even combed her hair when she was depressed. Things just spiraled down from there.

* * *

During this time, fruit was a big deal to us. Fresh fruit, in particular, was a luxury.

Mom used to send us to the store for her all the time. If she needed something for dinner or when she had a craving, Lynn and I would walk to the local market to get it. One night she asked us to get her more of her Spanish peanuts.

It was cold and had rained for several days. I didn't have a winter coat, so I borrowed Mom's big red coat, and I probably looked ridiculous. I was a size three and Mom was a size twenty-seven, so it hung on me. The arms were huge, and I had to constantly pull them up to use my hands. I couldn't roll them up because the material was made of thick wool. I should have known something was going to happen. Whenever Mom's big red coat was involved, there was always trouble. Mom was extra generous this time because she said we could get something we wanted. We both looked at each other and said, at the same time, "Fruit." Mom never had fruit in the house, so it became one of those special treats that we looked forward to.

My friend Debbie gave me a hard time when I acted excited because she had apples at her house. Her mom always had a big bowl full of apples, bananas, and oranges. I remember thinking that when I became a mom, I would have a bowl just like that, and my kids could have an apple any time they wanted. I actually pictured my future kids coming into our imaginary kitchen and just naturally grabbing an apple out of an imaginary bowl.

Lynn and I walked to Lester's Market, which was a good ten blocks from the house. It was still raining; our hair was wet and flattened to our heads, and our feet were cold from the puddles we deliberately stepped in. We didn't own an umbrella and we didn't miss having one. Umbrellas were for rich ladies with fancy clothes and their hair all done up. As we walked, we talked about what fruit we were going to get. Lynn wanted pears, and I wanted apples. Since Lynn was the oldest, she won out. I was really disappointed and pouted the rest of the way, but Lynn didn't give in. She wanted pears just as much as I wanted apples.

When we got to Lester's Market, we were soaked. We picked up Mom's peanuts first and then went to the fruit section. Lester's Market was your typical neighborhood market of its time. Its shelves contained nothing fancy, only canned goods and sundries. One section had nuts, chips and candy, and a large glass case in the back displayed meats, seafood, and salads. Towards the front, there was a large area for produce. The fruit was on one side, and the vegetables were on the other.

It was winter, so there weren't many fruits in season. There were bananas, apples, oranges, and pears. Lynn picked about six pears and put them in a paper bag. I took one look at the apples, and I wanted to cry because they looked so *good.* I must have stood there forever before I decided to do what any twelve-year-old girl would do in desperate times: I slipped two apples into the sleeve of the big, red coat. I kept my arms upright so the apples didn't slip out, and I made sure to walk slowly and carefully. I thought I was so clever, and I felt sure I could pull it off.

We got to the checkout stand, where Lester, the owner, was the only other person in the store. He was a really nice man who always wore a green apron, had grey hair, and he smiled in a way that lit up his face. He was friendly and made conversation with everyone. He asked us what we were doing out in this weather. Lynn proceeded to pay for the peanuts and the pears while I just stood there, anxious to leave. My hair was plastered to my face, but I couldn't fix it because I was trying hard not to move my arms. Lynn finished paying.

Just as I turned toward the door, the two apples I was trying to steal fell out from under my sleeves and rolled across the floor. Lester looked down at the apples and then up at me. I didn't know what to do. I took off running as fast as I could. He yelled, "Hey you!" and ran after me. I don't know how long he ran; I never looked back.

Poor Lynn didn't know I was taking the apples, and I left her there by herself. When she finally caught up with me she yelled at me for leaving her and asked what I thought I was doing. I was shaking and breathing really hard. I was so scared. I'd never stolen anything before and thought to myself, *If this is what it feels like to steal, I swear to never do it again.* I asked Lynn what Lester said to her when he got back to the store. She said that he wasn't really mad, more disappointed. He asked if she had known that I took the apples, and she told him that she hadn't. Then he just shook his head, which made me feel even worse than I already did.

Mom was lying on the couch watching television when we walked in. We were soaking wet, so we took our coats off and hung them on the back of the dining room chairs. When Lynn handed Mom her peanuts and the change, Mom asked what kind of fruit we got. Lynn showed her the pears, and Mom asked why we didn't get apples since she knew I loved them. Lynn told her that we only had enough money for pears. Mom said, "Why didn't you get half pears and half apples?" Lynn and I looked at each other. Why didn't we think of that? It never entered our minds that we could get both.

We didn't go back to Lester's Market for a long time. We went to another market that was several blocks further away. We really didn't have a choice; we didn't want to face Lester again. Even today, forty-plus years later, I still wish I could go back and apologize to Lester.

CHAPTER 6

Changes

It was embarrassing being poor. Everyone seemed to know.

Mom still had trouble paying the bills, and we didn't have anything left that could be repossessed. Whenever Mom was late paying her electricity or telephone bill, she would make us call (if our phone was still connected) or go down to the office in person. Most of the time, the people working at those places were really nice and would work out a payment plan for us. We hated doing it, but it always seemed to work.

I was embarrassed to go to school because my clothes were old and ugly. I wore Lynn's hand-me-downs, which were handed down from Arlene. By the time I got them, they were so outdated and worn out. We qualified for reduced lunches at school, but that was equally embarrassing because we had to stand in a special line. I would have rather gone hungry than stand in that line; they might as well have tattooed "needy" on our foreheads.

Mom took advantage of all the special programs that were offered. The welfare program gave out blocks of American cheese, butter, flour, dried beans, peanut butter, rice and other commodities, and we really needed that extra food. We made grilled cheese sandwiches with the cheese and butter, and rice and beans were a complete meal. The only thing I didn't like was when Mom made us go with her to pick up the food. It never failed—we always ran into someone from school. One time a girl from my high school was there helping her mom with distribution. She was not the nicest girl at school, and from that day on she treated me differently, like I had a disease.

Mom used to say, "There's nothing wrong with being poor. We haven't done anything wrong."

But when you're a kid, it's hard enough fitting in during the good times.

* * *

Late in 1964, when I was eleven years old, Mom and Dad separated. My father's first priority was not his family. He still came to our apartment, though, whenever he felt like it. We just never knew when he would be there, and he was usually drunk.

Dad used to drink and drive all the time. Mom used to say, "That man is lucky he hasn't hit something."

One night after drinking, he got behind the wheel of his black and yellow 1955 Chevy, drove down our street, and managed to hit every parked car on the block. He then parked, went into the house and went to bed. The next morning there was a knock on the door. A police officer arrested Dad for drunk and reckless driving. The police officer noted that Dad had managed to park his own car perfectly.

* * *

It was mostly just us girls living in the old, two-bedroom apartment, so extended family was unknown to me. When Mom and Dad left New York in 1954, they didn't look back. They didn't keep in touch with their parents or siblings. Neither one of them talked about family, so I never questioned if I had other family members like grandparents, uncles, aunts, or cousins.

But when Dad's older sister Rose and her daughter Joanie came to visit from New York for a couple of weeks, Mom made room. Dad moved back, making the appearance of caring for his family. It was strange. These people were family, and yet they felt like strangers. The worst part was that they acted superior to us. I was only a kid, but I felt it.

Aunt Rose took Joanie out for ice cream, and they actually came back to the house to eat it. Joanie was an only child who was a spoiled brat. I remember her commenting on how good her ice cream was and savoring every bit in front of us. It was obvious we never got ice cream. My younger sister Linda was only seven years old (and I don't think she remembered what ice cream tasted like), but I saw the wanting in her face, and I hated Joanie for it. After that, I did everything I could to avoid her.

Mom tried to encourage us to play with Joanie. "You girls need to take Joanie outside to play," she'd say. "Show her your paper dolls."

There is no way I'm going to let that little brat touch my precious paper dolls, I thought.

I hid them under the dresser and acted ignorant if anyone asked where they were.

The last straw came when Aunt Rose told Mom that I stole a dime. I think Mom wanted to keep the peace, so she said she believed Aunt Rose. "But I didn't take it!" I screamed. "I never even saw it!"

Aunt Rose swore that she put it on the counter and that I was the last one she saw in the kitchen. I cried tears of frustration and was sent to my room without dinner. I hated this so-called family and just wanted them to go home. They were mean, selfish, and ugly.

* * *

On a different occasion, Aunt Rose and her husband were again visiting from New York. They and my parents had been drinking all night, and when they got home, their voices seemed louder than normal.

Nights were always the worst. Bad things seemed to happen at night. Sounds were scarier and shadows that weren't there during the day just showed up at night. Trips to the bathroom were tough; my sisters and I always went in pairs because we were scared. Sometimes we would rather hold it in than go by ourselves. Even when we went in pairs, we had to pass the stairs, which were dark and steep. It was like demons lived on those stairs.

My parents fought more at night than at any other time, mainly because they were drinking; they drank all day and fought all night. We used to stay in our room, until eventually they would pass out and the house would get quiet.

On this particular night, when the four adults got home, it sounded like someone was physically fighting, and someone was screaming. I wasn't going to venture out to see what was happening. I just stayed put and figured I would find out in the morning. When morning came, my sisters and I went downstairs. We thought everyone was asleep but soon realized the house was empty. That was a nice reprieve for us. We relaxed and actually went outside to play, which we did for a while until a large, black car pulled up in front of our apartment.

A man and a woman, both dressed in black, got out of the car and asked our names. When they found out who we were, they told us that our parents were not coming home right away, and we were to lock up and go with them. In those days we didn't even think to question who they were or whether or not we should go with them. We just locked up the house and got in their car. They drove us to a place called Hillcrest Receiving Home in downtown San Diego. It was a place children were taken when they had no one to care for them.

I remember being scared at first. *Where are we? How long will we be here? Will I be with my sisters? Who should I trust?*

But once we were settled and realized we were going to be staying there a while, I actually fell in love with the place. It was so well structured.

I loved how we had to keep our rooms clean. They had the prettiest chenille bedspreads; mine was pink. I remember feeling safe there. They had a point system, and we got extra points for everything positive we did. If we worked in the kitchen, we got points; if we worked in the nursery, we got points. These points were added up at the end of the week, and then we got to go to "The Closet."

The Closet was just that, a closet filled with donated items we could buy with our points. There were stuffed animals, coloring books and crayons, ceramic knickknacks, and other stuff we could use to decorate our rooms.

We also lined up for meals, and the meals were wonderful. I was so excited to have fresh fruit and vegetables. For some reason my mother bought only canned vegetables and fruit, even plums. Once, after she made canned corned beef, a neighbor came to visit and found all of us deathly sick. A doctor had to make a house call because we were all too ill to travel to the hospital. The doctor said we were lucky the neighbor found us because we had food poisoning that could have been fatal.

At Hillcrest, I also learned to play Ping Pong, and I got really good. I perfected a serve that challenged some of the best players I knew.

I would have preferred to stay at Hillcrest forever than go home to our living hell.

We found out later that my mother tried to kill my father by going after him with a knife, and the neighbors called the police. My father was taken to jail, and my mother was committed to a mental hospital, where she stayed for several months. My father was released and went back to live on the ship.

We stayed at Hillcrest while the state petitioned to have us placed as "Wards of the Court" for our protection. As wards of the court, if our parents could not continue to care for us, we could be placed in another receiving home, in foster care, or in an adoption situation. We were appointed a caseworker who had our files and information.

With just a phone call, we would be removed from our home and placed elsewhere instantly. Periodically, the caseworker was required to check up on us and update her files as to our condition and the condition of the home we were living in.

My mother was eventually released from the hospital. We went to court and were released back into Mom's custody. And so life continued.

* * *

Parents are supposed to protect their children at all costs. When I hear about adults that know they are putting their children in harm's way but continue on that path of destruction, I wonder, *What are they thinking?* Obviously, they are not. My mom was no exception. She loved my dad so much that for years she justified and made excuses for his behavior.

But finally, after years of his abuse and neglect (and then the visit from his relatives), something triggered in Mom and she snapped. I found out why she went after him with a knife that night.

When Mom married Dad, my oldest sister Arlene (from Mom's previous marriage) was seven years old. Soon after, my mom sent her to live with Aunt Gertie in New York City. For years, I never understood why she did that because my mother's family was so prejudiced against Arlene's Asian father. Her family never accepted the marriage or Arlene, so when Mom sent her there, she was badly treated. Uncle Bobby, who was only a few years older than Arlene, was the worst.

He fed her dog food, was hostile, and called her a "Chink." Aunt Gertie did nothing to stop his behavior. In fact, whenever she had company, she would have Arlene come into the room and tell her to "show them your monkey ears."

Arlene had to endure their hostility for several years before finally returning home when she was thirteen. Arlene was such a beautiful little girl and even more beautiful as a teenager. It soon became clear to all of us why Arlene was sent away: my father was a child molester. My mother knew it shortly after they were married, and her only alternative was to remove Arlene from the house. Why didn't she just get rid of *him*? I don't know why Arlene came back home. He left her alone while we lived in Tennessee but when we moved to our new house in California, he would come home drunk and go after her. She would have to barricade herself in her room and move her dresser in front of the door.

We could hear her screaming. Where was Mom? Why wasn't she doing something? Lynn, Linda, and I didn't dare leave our room. The fact that we shared a room was what kept him away from us. Arlene ended up pregnant and married at age seventeen to her high school sweetheart. She moved away and never looked back. I remember thinking she was the lucky one.

* * *

The sixties came and went in a blink; my life was so hectic. Between men coming to take away the few things we had and making a new home for ourselves at Hillcrest, it makes sense that somehow I missed "the sixties."

In the movie *Field of Dreams*, Kevin Costner's wife says, "You experienced two fifties and moved right into the seventies."

That was me! I lived through them but never really *experienced* them. I missed the hippie era, Jimmy Hendrix, and Janice Joplin. I do remember going to my friend Chris' house and listening to The Beatles' *White Album*. She spent every penny she ever earned on records, and when she showed them to me, I didn't recognize most of them. I even missed the current events. I was working for an accountant in 1974 when someone mentioned Charles Manson and I asked, "Who is that?" I had never heard the story of the crazed man and his followers who killed all those people, including Sharon Tate and her unborn baby, even though it was on every news channel and in every magazine and newspaper.

Woodstock was another event I didn't hear about until much later. Someone asked me if I would have gone to Woodstock if I had the chance. I didn't know what to say because the sixties were a complete blur to me. They were years of me just trying to survive my childhood. Mom and Dad were always drinking and fighting. We had moved continuously. Money had been tight with Dad's gambling. His family from hell came to visit, which eventually led us to Hillcrest where there was no TV and no one listened to the radio.

I've talked to so many people who felt for some reason or another that they had also missed the sixties. People were busy raising families, earning a living, or attending school and weren't able to experience the freedom of expression and craziness of that time. Since then, there has been so much hype on television and in the movies, but how many really experienced "the sixties" as they're now remembered? How many people were like me, just trying to survive?

CHAPTER 7

Sixth Grade

It was my sixth grade year and my sixth elementary school. Always being the new kid on the block was hard. I never had enough time to make friends, so I dreaded the first day of school. Everyone seemed excited about seeing their old friends from last year, but I found myself standing off to the side or sitting way in the back in the chair no one wanted.

But this year was different; this year I had Mrs. Carter as my teacher. She made all her students feel like they were the best and most important. Even while she was making one person feel special, she made everyone else a part of what she was doing.

Mrs. Carter had shoulder-length, sandy-blonde hair, and she wore matching skirts with cardigan sweaters. I remember thinking that she looked so nice and neat. We became instant friends. She moved me to the front of the classroom and gave me the important classroom assignments, like taking the roll to the office, keeping score while playing games, or passing out papers during class. I loved everything about that school year.

The principal was retiring after many years. She had done a lot of nice things at our school, so they were re-naming it in her honor. Our class was in charge of a special presentation for her, and Mrs. Carter chose me to present her with flowers at the graduation.

This was such a special occasion, as well as my sixth grade graduation, so Mom took me shopping for a new outfit. I'll never forget it. It was a two-piece, double-breasted, baby blue seersucker suit with a pleated skirt. It was the most beautiful outfit I had ever owned, and Mom surprised me with a pair of nylons and a pretty white garter belt to hold them up. It felt like a dream.

The night before graduation day, I laid out everything I was going to wear. I kept looking at it, thinking that any minute someone was going to take it. We rarely got anything new, and then Mom had a bad habit of giving our stuff away. I remember one day we came home from school and Mom had given away our dining room table and chairs. (She met a large family she felt needed it more than we did.) It wasn't the nicest dining set, but it was the only one we had. We ended up eating on the floor or from our laps.

Back in the fourth grade, I had won an autograph book for writing the best scary story, and I still didn't have many autographs in it besides the cherished one from Bill. But I knew that after tomorrow, my book would be full.

The next morning, I woke up so excited that I didn't want to eat breakfast. I just wanted to get dressed and go to school. I couldn't wait for Mrs. Carter to see my new clothes. Mom was in the kitchen drinking coffee when I came in; she knew how excited I was and wanted me to have a great day.

She saw that I had my autograph book with me and asked if I had a pen so everyone could sign it. I hadn't even thought of a pen. She pointed to a side drawer and told me to use hers. I knew which pen she was talking about and couldn't believe my luck. That was my mom's favorite pen. Someone had given it to her, and it had always been off-limits for any of us to use. Now she was letting me take it to school.

Her special pen was silver, and on the side where she clipped it to her pocket was a pair of praying hands. It must have been really valuable. This was my special day, and everything was going well. We lived only a couple of blocks from the school, so I walked. Mom said she would see me at the graduation.

Our class spent all morning preparing. I practiced when and how to present the flowers, and Mrs. Carter really loved my new outfit—she had a way of making me feel pretty. We were allowed some time for autograph signing and visiting, and soon my book was almost filled with autographs. It felt good to make friends, and some of the girls wrote encouraging things like "Let's get together this summer" or "It was fun knowing you." Some even gave me their phone numbers and told me to call them. Most of the boys just signed their names, but my book was pretty full, and I couldn't wait to read what everyone had written. Then it was time.

We put all our stuff away and walked in a single-file line to the outside playground, where the ceremony would be held. All the parents were there, and although my mom sat in the back, I saw her, and she waved. She looked happy, which made me beam inside.

Everything went perfectly. I walked up and presented the principal with her flowers and walked back without any problems. (I had pictured myself falling flat on my face, but that didn't happen.) The graduation was a success. Mom went home; I told her I would help my teacher clean up and that I'd see her later.

We all helped put up chairs and pick up papers. The wonderful school year was over. I didn't want it to end, but at the same time I was excited about junior high school. I went to get my sweater and autograph book.

My autograph book was there, but where was the pen? Where was that precious pen, that pen my mom entrusted me with? I searched everywhere. I moved everything moveable, but it was gone. I was heartsick and scared. Mom loved that pen. I didn't know what to do, and I didn't want to go home and have to face her.

I started to cry. I knew I needed to face the music, confess to losing her pen, and take the punishment. More than being afraid of punishment, I didn't want to ruin my mom's day. She had looked so proud and happy at the graduation—now I was going to shatter all of that. I slowly walked home and cried all the way.

Mom had a way of overreacting at even the smallest things. I remember when I was younger and tripped over something on the floor while carrying a platter of meat. The meat went everywhere—and of course, it was an accident—but she went ballistic and started hitting me with her fist over and over again. When she got mad and started hitting, she never knew when to stop. It was like she was out of control; she hit us with whatever she had in her hand at the time, and on that occasion, I was lucky it was only her fist.

When I got close to home, I really started to cry. I turned into the driveway and saw my mom. She was smiling, talking to our neighbor, and bragging about how wonderful the graduation had been—what a good job I had done presenting the flowers.

Mom took one look at me and knew something was wrong. She looked scared; she couldn't imagine what could have happened to make me cry that hard. I just stood there because I didn't know how to tell her. She took me in her arms, and we went inside the house. She gently sat me down and asked what had happened and why was I crying. I just looked at her and said, "I lost your pen."

By this time I was trembling. I just started crying harder and harder until I could barely breathe. I looked at my mom, not knowing what the severity of my punishment would be.

"What pen?" she asked.

"Your favorite pen in the world," I sobbed. She still looked puzzled.

"The praying hands pen!" I said more urgently.

"Oh, that old thing?" she asked, confused. "It's okay."

I couldn't believe it. "But you never let us touch that pen. It was your favorite," I said, bewildered.

"I never let you touch it because it was the only pen in the house," she said with a laugh. "I can always get another pen. Is that what this is all about?" She hugged me again and got up as if nothing had happened.

I just sat there. Exhausted, I fell asleep in the chair.

* * *

Our neighbor's Siamese cat had kittens. Mom said I could have one if I agreed to take care of it. I picked a boy and named him Smokey because he was several shades of grey, black, and white. He was beautiful. I kept to my word and took care that Smokey was house-trained and didn't chew or claw on anything.

I made claw toys and string toys to play with him. I, of course, got attached; this was only my second pet. The first was my puppy that was hit by a truck. I watched Smokey closely and made sure he was home at night since he was an indoor and outdoor cat that roamed the neighborhood.

One day he came home with a wound in his side. At first I thought he had been in a fight with another cat. When the wound wouldn't heal, I talked Mom into taking him to the pet hospital. The doctor said that Smokey had a foxtail embedded in his side and they would need to do minor surgery to remove it. I was worried. I talked Mom into paying for the surgery. It was $134.00.

I remember because I told Mom I would pay her back. I was young but responsible, and planned to babysit for a neighbor in order to pay Mom back every penny. Mom reluctantly agreed to the surgery, although she had a hard time with it. She thought $134.00 was too much to spend on a pet. I stayed at the hospital and waited for Smokey, and then we took him home. He healed really well.

Smokey never liked Mom. I think animals can sense when someone doesn't like them. During this time, Mom was a nurse's aide at a local hospital. She wore a white uniform with white stockings and white shoes, and Smokey started going to the bathroom in her shoes. When Mom would get ready for work, she would slip her shoes on and scream, "Mary!"

I did everything to try and get Smokey not to pee in Mom's shoes. I tried to always keep her door closed. She left her shoes at the bottom of her closet, which she always kept closed, but Smokey was relentless and he always found a way in. Mom finally got so mad that one day while I was at school, she took him and dropped him off somewhere. I never saw Smokey again.

I pleaded with her to take me to him. I waited for weeks, thinking he would make his way back to me, but he never came back. I never had another pet after Smokey. I never wanted to get attached to another animal.

I realized years later that Smokey would pee in Mom's shoes after she yelled or punished me for something. He was protecting me, and I wish I had realized what he was doing. I would have rewarded him for a job well done.

* * *

Although my parents weren't legally divorced in 1965, Dad stayed away for a while, and that made things more peaceful at home. Mom started dating. She dated quite a few guys while we were growing up, but only one stands out as my favorite. His name was Sonny, and he was in the Navy. I think I had a crush on him; he had blonde hair and blue eyes. He was from Georgia and had a Southern accent that made him even more likeable.

Sonny wasn't one of those men who were always trying to hug or kiss us like most of the ones Mom dated. He was a genuinely nice guy. He smiled a lot and made everyone feel good. I remember thinking he was too nice for Mom.

Mom was always in a good mood when Sonny was around. The house came alive and there was more talking and laughing. Normally, I stayed in my room. Mom was usually angry about something, but not now—not while Sonny was around. Now I could come out of my room, watch TV, play rummy, or just talk. It was wonderful.

Mom dated Sonny longer than most. I remember Sonny went to Australia. When he returned, he had gifts for all of us. He brought stuffed animals for Lynn and Linda, and he brought me a stuffed koala bear. I had never heard of a koala before, so he brought me information about it.

Sonny always took the time to talk to us. He didn't dismiss us like most adults, but acted sincerely interested in what we did at school. He even offered to help us with our homework. Once he helped me with a science project; I don't remember what the project was, but I do remember getting a good grade. He was excited for me and took us all out for hamburgers. He was genuinely interested in how things were going in our lives. It was wonderful having Sonny around, and I looked forward to seeing him every time he came to visit.

Unfortunately, something happened, and Mom quit dating Sonny. I asked Mom why Sonny wasn't coming over anymore, but all she said was, "We got into a fight, and he really pissed me off."

I hoped they would make up and he would come back. But that didn't happen, and Mom started going to the bars again.

* * *

The door to the Corral was held open by a wooden doorstop to keep the air flowing. Inside the doorway there was a heavy black curtain to keep the light out. I stood there for several minutes, my eyes adjusting to the darkness. The smell was always the same—stale beer and overflowing ashtrays. Once my eyes adjusted, I quickly looked to find her sitting in her favorite seat. The same people (as always) were sitting on either side of her, the same old music playing on the jukebox. There was no conversation, and everyone looked to be deep in thought. It felt so depressing.

My sisters and I always took turns when we had to get Mom from the bar. It was my turn; it was only fair.

Mom was sitting with her head down, so it took her a few minutes to realize I was standing at the door. I didn't dare go in; I knew she'd really be mad if I did that. When she finally noticed me, she motioned for me to come over. I was nervous. This time she didn't look mad; she just looked sad. She looked at me and said softly, "You girls ready to go home?" I nodded my head. She left some money on the bar, and we both walked quietly to the car.

Mom was sad for a long time.

I wasn't sure what I preferred: when she was mad (which meant yelling and hitting) or when she was sad (which meant she just laid around feeling sorry for herself). I think I preferred the yelling and hitting. It was painful but short lived; she yelled, hit, and it was over. Being sad lasted for days, maybe even weeks. The whole house was under a dark cloud—no life, just the sadness. Either way, we suffered. I remember thinking, "Why do people drink?"

* * *

Mom always had her boyfriends behind locked doors in her bedroom. We knew not to disturb her when she had company.

It was Sunday night and we were watching Disney. The Mouseketeers were on first and then a Disney special. Annette Funicello was my favorite Mouseketeer because she always reminded me of my sister Arlene. They wore their hair in the same bobbed style, ratted on top. Annette had the same walk and body shape as Arlene. I thought Arlene was so beautiful. Arlene went to the beach with her friends just like Annette and Frankie in all those beach party movies, which I loved.

We were lying on the floor in the living room when the front door opened and Dad walked in. He was in his white Navy uniform, with a six-pack of beer under one arm, and a six-pack of Coke under the other. We froze. We knew Mom had company, and that Dad wasn't supposed to be there (although he always just showed up whenever he felt like it). It had been at least six months since we last saw him. We didn't know what to do.

He set down the beer and Coke, took off his white sailor hat and threw it on the table. "Where's your mom?" he asked, nonchalantly.

He knew from the looks on our faces that something was wrong. He turned and glanced in the direction of her bedroom then back at us. He knew she was in her room, and he knew she was not alone. He asked, "Who's in there?"

We just sat silently. What were we supposed to say? He picked up his hat, put it back on his head, picked up the beer and Coke, and left.

Lynn went and knocked on Mom's door. A few minutes later, Mom came out wearing her slip. She always reminded me of those World War II wives in the movies who walked around in curlers, bright red lipstick and a full-length slip. "What's going on?" she asked. Lynn explained that Dad was just there and he left mad.

She told us to run after him. "Stop him. Don't let him leave mad."

We did what she told us to do. All three of us ran out the door and down the street. He was walking and didn't stop, so we ran in front of him.

We pleaded with him, "Dad, please don't be mad. Mom asked us to tell you she's sorry and please not to be mad."

We didn't know what else to say. He couldn't come back to the house because she still had company. An angry look was fixed on his face, and he kept walking. We finally turned around and went back home. It was freezing outside; none of us had jackets on. Linda was shivering. I remember thinking that adults made so many problems for themselves. I also realized he hadn't left the six-pack of Coke. Those Cokes were for us. He was mad at Mom, so he was going to punish us, too. I remember thinking, *Heck, he can leave, but just leave us the Coke.*

Years later, I found out that when Dad would just pop in like that, he would give Mom money. It's like he paid her for sex, and she really looked forward to that extra money. So that night she wasn't upset because he left; she just wanted to make sure that he came back.

CHAPTER 8

Junior High School

In 1966, when one of your children needed his or her tonsils out, it seemed like the doctor just removed all the children's tonsils in that family. I was thirteen years old and was experiencing a sore throat and earache all the time. Since Mom was on Medi-Cal, the doctor thought it would be more economical for my sister, Lynn, to have her tonsils out as well. Lynn was fine and didn't need her tonsils out, but the doctor said she would eventually, so we might as well remove hers, too. We were both booked for the same time, and we shared a room. The doctor made it seem like it was going to be fun. He even said we couldn't go to school for a whole week, and we could have all the ice cream we wanted.

I remember being really excited. I'd never been in a hospital before, and the fact that Lynn was going also just made it that much more fun. We checked in, and the nurse gave us matching hospital gowns to put on. We jumped onto our beds and were wheeled down the hall to an elevator and up a couple of floors to what we assumed was the operating room. I smiled over at Lynn, but she didn't smile back. Did she know something I didn't?

When we woke up in our room, we were both very sick and throwing up. I made it to the bowl they gave us, but Lynn threw up all over the floor. My throat felt like someone took sandpaper and scrubbed it raw. We were both in so much pain that it hurt too much to talk. This was not what I thought it was going to be like. I knew we'd be a little sore, but I thought we'd be able to talk and watch TV while eating all the ice cream we wanted. What a gyp! Who the heck wants ice cream when you felt as awful as we did?

* * *

I had just started the seventh grade. We moved into another house, and I hadn't had time to make friends. The first day of school was scary. Not only was this a different school, but it was junior high. I met a girl named Helen the first day, and we became instant friends. I invited her to a sleepover at my house, and I was so excited because this was the first time I'd ever had a friend spend the night. We were sharing my twin bed; I was at one end and she was at the other.

We were both fast asleep when something woke me. I looked up and saw my dad sitting on the bed, staring at Helen. What was he doing in my room? He wasn't even supposed to be at our house. I looked down at Helen, and she looked frightened. Dad had been drinking. I immediately said, "Dad, what are you doing in here?" but he didn't say a thing. He didn't even look at me. He just got up and staggered out of the room. Helen and I didn't say anything to each other. I was mortified, and she looked scared. Dad was creepy when he drank. He didn't even look like the same person.

His eyes were glazed with lust and he had been staring at her with evil in his heart. What was he doing in my room? He had never come into my room before. Mom must have mentioned I had a friend over. What if I hadn't woken up? What if he had done something to her? Touched her? This is something that haunts a person; this could have damaged Helen for life. I was embarrassed and frightened.

Helen never spent the night again. I never invited her, and she never asked. We hung out at school, and I would go to her house every once in a while, but she never came to mine. We never talked about it.

We moved again the next year. I went to a different junior high school for the next two years. I didn't see Helen until high school. We were cordial with each other, but by this time we hung out in different circles.

Even though Dad didn't touch her, his actions still did damage. Because of my dad, Helen lost a little of her innocence that night.

I've never forgotten. Other events and my mom's confessions confirmed the fear I had. My dad was an evil man, and he hurt a lot of innocent children, but he was never punished for his crimes. I probably don't know half of what he did in his life, but I do know that he died a sick and miserable man.

* * *

"Reggie." Even the name brings back sweet memories.

Seventh grade was a time of innocence. I hung out with a small group of friends from junior high school. We walked to the roller skate rink on Saturday mornings. It was early when we arrived—not a lot of kids were there yet—so we had the rink to ourselves. I was just an okay skater with no backward skating skills or fancy footwork. I felt lucky to be steady on my feet. But I skated around and around, like I didn't have a care in the world.

Life was semi-peaceful for me. Dad was gone, and Mom was happily dating again. As I skated, I felt someone slowly take my hand. I looked down and then over at Reggie. I was in heaven. We were young and clumsy; I didn't know what to do. We didn't talk, just skated around, but I felt like the luckiest girl alive. Reggie was such a good-looking kid. He had moved into the neighborhood about the same time we did, and he lived with his mom and sister. He had the most adorable baby face and the biggest dimples. He was a really nice guy, too. We had a similar family life: his mother drank and got violent at times. I remember one incident when Reggie had gotten in trouble for something, and his mother went ballistic, hitting him over and over again. He was then sent to his room. My sisters and I went to his bedroom window to talk to him, and we saw how he was trying to be brave. I knew he was hurting, but he tried to act like he was okay. I felt so bad for him—maybe because I could relate.

We hung out at school and became friends. When he took my hand that day, I can still remember how excited I felt because he picked *me* when he could have picked any of the other girls. Nothing ever came of our relationship besides holding hands. We never even kissed.

Reggie moved away for a few years and returned in our senior year. I didn't think it was possible, but he looked even better, more mature, and was cuter than ever. We dated a couple of times, but stayed just as friends. I know he married a girl from school after she got pregnant. They had three daughters, but the last I heard was they were divorced. I was so sad to hear that. He was like the rest of us; he had dreams and expectations.

I think about Reggie every once in a while and wonder if life has been good to him. Did he go down the same path our parents led? Or did he make his own way? Whatever he did, I hope he was happy. He was a really nice guy.

* * *

Mom started dating another guy whose name was Eddie. Eddie was a charmer. Everyone liked him, so when they began dating, her friends were all excited that she had finally found someone who could make her happy. Most of the guys she dated were heavy drinkers and hung out in bars, but Eddie was different. He wanted to spend more time at our house and do things with the family. Eddie even took us shopping and out to eat.

I was getting ready to go into the eighth grade, and I needed some new clothes. Mom announced that Eddie was taking us shopping. We went to a department store where I was told I could buy a new dress and a pair of shoes. I picked a yellow and navy blue plaid shirtdress that was the latest fashion. But I was torn between two pairs of shoes: one was a pair of navy blue pumps that would go with other clothes I had at home, and the other was a pair of shiny yellow patent leather pumps. They looked so good sitting on the shelf; they came in several different colors, but I couldn't take my eyes off the yellow pair. I had to have them.

Why didn't Mom talk me out of them? How could she let me leave the store with those shoes? When we got home, I went right in to try on my new outfit. I came out to model my clothes and I thought my sisters would rave about how great I looked, but everyone just stared at me, unable to keep their eyes off my shoes. When I went back in my room to change, it hit me that I had made a really terrible mistake. I should have picked the navy blue pumps.

Now what? I had to wear them because they were the only shoes I had. I would have to wear them every day.

The first day of school arrived, and my best friend Cindy came to walk to school with me. She saw my shoes and started to laugh; she thought they were horrible, and I wanted to cry. Cindy had really weird taste, so I thought for sure she would like my yellow shoes. But when even she hated them, I knew I had made a bad choice.

At school, I knew I looked ridiculous, and I saw kids staring at my shoes all day. Everyday, people could see me from across the campus. I told myself that I would never again be so quick to buy the first thing that caught my eye. I learned a lesson that day, and I started babysitting to save the money to buy a new pair of navy blue pumps.

Eddie was a middle-aged man, probably around forty-five years old. He had never been married. He stood about five feet, ten inches tall and weighed 250 pounds or more. I remember him being fat and sloppy. He wore T-shirts that were tight around the middle with his belly sticking out. I never knew what Mom liked about him except that he was a nice guy. Maybe that was the attraction. "It's hard to find a really nice guy," I'd hear her say.

Mom wasn't drinking as much now that she and Eddie were dating. So when she said we were going to the drive-in to see *The Sound of Music*, I was excited. There were always promises of going to the movies or going to the beach, but we never went. I remember thinking, *I really like Eddie.*

I was the only one at home at the time, so I got the whole back seat of his 1959 Buick to myself. We got to the Harbor Drive-in and settled in. Mom fell asleep almost immediately. She always fell asleep during a movie or while watching TV. Everything was perfect until I felt a hand touch my leg. I was startled because I didn't even see him move. Eddie was facing the movie screen but had managed to reach in the back seat.

At first I thought he was just going to pat my leg, but then his hand started up my inner thigh, and he proceeded to stretch his fingers, trying to open my legs. I was panicked; I moved to the other side of the car, but still he found a way to touch me. He kept clawing at me, trying to get inside my pants. He was stronger than me, and I honestly didn't know what to do. I wanted to scream out to my mom, but I was afraid to wake her and also afraid of ruining everything for her. Mom was finally happy. I kept moving away from his probing hands. I kept thinking, *Why is he doing this?*

I finally moved up inside the back window of the car. I flattened myself, facing away from him against the window. He continued reaching for me, but I was far enough away that he could barely touch me. Nevertheless, he was relentless and continued to try. I think he enjoyed the sport of it. He knew I was frightened, and that excited him. Scared to death, I stayed flattened against the back window of the car during the entire movie. I never watched the movie—just prayed that he would stop or Mom would wake up and we could go home. When Mom finally did wake up, she didn't even question why I was in the window, facing the opposite direction. We stayed until the movie was finished and then we went home.

I never said anything about that night to anyone. I just stayed away from Eddie. Mom and Eddie stopped dating shortly after that, and we never saw him again. I think I was in my thirties when I finally told Mom about that night. She was horrified.

"Why didn't you tell me?" she asked.

I said, "You were so happy, and I didn't want to spoil it for you."

Her eyes filled with tears. Eddie knew Mom was lonely, and he knew she had young daughters. He charmed his way into our home and into our lives. Money was tight, and I have to admit—I loved that yellow and navy blue plaid shirtdress. I wore it until it fell apart.

* * *

Dad was back in our lives again. I don't know why Mom let him move back in with us, but she did. Nothing had changed. They were both still drinking and fighting.

One night I was fast asleep until I felt someone softly nudging me. It took me a few minutes to wake up and realize it was my mom. What was she doing in our bedroom? It was still dark outside; the moon was peeking through the curtains. I could see that Mom was wearing her big red coat. It was funny, but every time Mom wore that coat, something awful happened. The coat's red wool was faded, and it had a large collar and fell to mid-calf, making her look overweight and sloppy. I always hated that coat, but she seemed to wear it whenever she was passionate about something. She had her finger to her lips as if to say, "Shhh, be quiet." My two sisters were slowly moving around the room, trying to find their shoes. Mom told us to quietly get dressed.

I asked her, "Where are we going?"

She whispered, "I will tell you later. Just get dressed and be quiet."

She said that Dad was passed out in the other room, and we didn't want to wake him. When we all had our coats on, she led us outside.

We walked single-file behind Mom. We lived on a street that had gravel and blacktop. We walked as though we were tiptoeing, careful not to kick the gravel, until we were far enough away from the house so that we could walk normally. Each one of us was in our own thoughts, and it was cold and dark. I knew something was seriously wrong. I wasn't sure if I really wanted to know what was happening; I had a feeling it was bad.

Whatever was happening had something to do with my older sister, Lynn. Lynn was fourteen years old, I was thirteen, and my youngest sister Linda was nine. I thought all teenagers were difficult, but lately Lynn had seemed genuinely depressed. She was crying a lot and not talking to anyone. I had overheard Lynn and Mom talking softly in the bedroom the night before Dad came home. I heard Mom whispering to someone on the phone, and then we were sent to bed.

We walked several miles before we got to Edna's house. Edna had been a friend of my mom's since we moved to San Diego. She was Mom's landlady, and they remained friends after we moved. Edna was divorced with two grown sons, and we spent a lot of time with her when Mom was looking for a job. Edna seemed to know we were coming because she opened the door before we got to it; she was crying when she hugged Mom and then hugged Lynn. Edna's house was warm. We took our coats off, hung them on a hook, and Mom told Linda and I to go back to bed. There were beds made up in Edna's spare room, and I was too tired to ask questions. I fell asleep instantly.

When I woke up the house was quiet. I knew that Edna was in the kitchen since I could smell the strong, delicious scent of coffee brewing. I was always disappointed that it never tasted the way it smelled. I stayed in bed as long as I could.

I didn't want to get up. I knew I would learn soon enough what was happening with Lynn, and I wanted to postpone it as long as possible.

Mom and Lynn came back after lunch. Mom took Linda and I into another room and asked us a lot of questions about Dad. She asked if Dad had ever hurt us, or if he had ever touched us in private places. Mom said Lynn had told her that Dad touched her and it was better if we told her the truth—that no one would be mad, that she just needed to know. I told her the truth: "No, he never touched me." Linda said that he had never touched her, either. Mom said "Okay," and never asked us again.

Things changed after that day. The police arrested Dad, although he didn't stay in jail for long. The Navy protected him, so he never got in trouble, but he never came home again. The judge ordered him to get counseling, and he said he would, but he never followed through.

Lynn changed forever. She lost her youthful glow and would never be the same. She fell in love at sixteen, got pregnant, quit school, and got married at seventeen.

Thirty years passed. After four failed marriages and many hours of therapy, Lynn was ready to face our dad. She was ready to ask that question that had haunted her all those years: "Why? Why me? Why was I singled out?"

She went to see our father at his home. He lived alone in a small, one-bedroom house. When he answered the door, it was as if he had been waiting for her, as if he knew this day would come. Lynn went in, sat down at his small kitchen table, looked him in the eye, and asked, "Why me?"

My father answered, "I don't know. I knew one day you would ask me this, and still I have no answer for you. I'm so sorry."

She looked down at this very frail, broken man, and all the hate she had felt was gone. She felt only pity for him now.

Several years later, my dad got sick. He had been a drinker and smoker his whole life, and now he was suffering the consequences of his choices. He had emphysema and was hooked up to an oxygen tank. He needed someone to look after him, and Lynn was the one who took him in. She quit her job and took care of him. When he died at the age of sixty-three, Lynn was at his side.

* * *

I met the five Lawson girls during the summer before eighth grade. The oldest, Karen, was seventeen; Debbie was fifteen, Cindy was thirteen, and Kathy was ten. Cindy and I had a lot of classes together. My sister Lynn hung out with Debbie and Karen. Linda and Kathy became friends, and they were just young enough to be the pesty, tag-along sisters. The Lawson girls all had red hair and freckles. They were outgoing and had no trouble getting the boys to pay attention to them; I always envied them for that.

Karen was dating an older boy named John Dawson. John introduced his friend Randy to Lynn, and they fell in love. They were inseparable. Lynn became pregnant at sixteen, dropped out of school, and married Randy. After Randy finished high school, he got a job at the local Volkswagen dealership. He worked his way up the ladder in the parts department, and eventually he and his brother Rick bought a Volkswagen repair shop called Peanuts.

Lynn and Randy had a son they also named Randy. Unfortunately, they divorced when Randy was two. They stayed good friends throughout the years and still see each other on special occasions.

Cindy and I were friends first, but after we got into a fight over something stupid and stopped hanging out, Debbie and I became close. We did everything together.

In 1967, everyone hitchhiked everywhere. Debbie and I never hitchhiked alone, but one time we were trying to get a ride home from school, as usual. Debbie stuck her thumb out, and a car pulled over really fast. Debbie didn't realize her dad was the driver, and he was so mad that I thought for sure we were dead. But she told him she knew it was him, and we were just playing. I'm still not sure he believed us, but since he worked long days at the steel mill to provide for his wife and five daughters, the poor man was exhausted. He pretended to believe us anyway and gave us a ride home.

We never had any money, so we had to come up with things to do that didn't require any. We played hopscotch, jumped rope, and wherever we could find a smooth surface, we played jacks.

I liked going to Debbie's house because her mom stayed home all day and they always had food. At our house we were lucky if we had bread. (Sometimes we would have mayonnaise sandwiches for dinner.) But Debbie's mom always cooked and baked, so it was fun to go to her house. I remember getting in trouble for skipping school. Mom found out, and I got really scared, so I ran away from home. I didn't run far; I hid in Debbie's closet.

They had the greatest old, gable-roofed house. The top floor was one large bedroom the girls all shared. It was so great because they could climb up a ladder from the back and get into their room without anyone knowing. When I ran away, Debbie's parents didn't know I was there. During the day while the girls were at school, I would have to be really quiet so their mom didn't hear me. At night they would sneak me food. It was fun at first, but then I got bored. My sisters came to see me. They told me that Mom was really sad, and that I should go home, so I did.

CHAPTER 9

Alotta's

"Money is tight!"

We were moving again for the second time in a year, and that was my mother's reasoning. Normally, we just went along with whatever Mom wanted; arguing only got us in trouble. We never really had a say in any of the decisions she made, anyway. "We're moving and that's that!" she would say. This time, however, I honestly resented her decision. I was a typical sixteen-year-old girl who was beginning to realize that I should have a say in my own life.

"I can't live here!" I cried, while Mom was showing us our new place of residence.

It was the summer before my junior year in high school. Mom was moving her three teenage daughters above a run-down, dirty old bar that was attached to a corner liquor store. It was the neighborhood hangout for all the regulars, as well as the stragglers, and had been around for years. It wasn't fancy or fixed up in any way. Alotta's was in a dull, brown, two-story building. The bottom floor was the bar and pizza parlor, with four small, two-bedroom apartments set above the restaurant. The front entrance was a door that led up a dark, narrow flight of stairs, and at the top of the stairs were two doors on each side. If you can think of the ugliest old bar imaginable, you're probably picturing Alotta's. How could I face my friends? I didn't want anyone to know where I lived.

"It's five dollars a month cheaper."

That was her excuse. But I knew the real reason we were moving to Alotta's: one of Mom's drinking buddies lived in the apartment next door, and Mom would not have to travel far to meet her. They could just walk down the stairs, drink all day, stagger back upstairs, and pass out in their own beds.

I imagined Mom saying to herself, *Wow, why didn't I think of this sooner? How clever. Forget for a moment that you have the safety and reputation of your three teenage daughters to consider. What's more important anyway, them or me?*

I thought that life couldn't get much worse. To top it all off, the school bus stop was at the same corner as Alotta's. The reputation that was attached to living above a bar was more than I could take. I went to extremes to hide where I was living. I didn't date anyone from school because dating meant the boy would want to know where I lived. I got up early every morning, just so I could walk several blocks in the opposite direction, turn around, and walk back toward the bus stop in order to avoid anyone seeing me descend the stairs of our apartment. I found out later that everyone knew I lived above Alotta's. I wasn't fooling anyone.

* * *

In 1969, we had just moved into the apartment above Alotta's, and the whole family, except for Dad, was there for Thanksgiving dinner. Lynn and Randy were married and expecting a baby in December. Arlene was with her second husband, Chris, and her two sons, Ricky (one) and Joey (five).

While dinner was in the oven, we all sat down to watch a movie on TV. It was a 1956 family film called *All Mine to Give*, starring Cameron Mitchell. It was based on a true story about a Scottish immigrant family with six children and their losing battle against the frontier of Wisconsin. After the father died, the mother (on her death bed) told the oldest boy that he needed to place each one of his brothers and sisters in a loving home. He promised to do this. The children were remarkable as they worked together to keep that promise. Pulling a wagon through the snow, the oldest boy placed each of his five siblings, one by one, into just the right family. The families he picked were loving and accepting, and each time he left one of his sisters or brothers, we could feel his heart breaking. What an incredible young man. After all the children were placed, the twelve-year-old boy pulled his sleigh up a hill in the snow on his way to work in the logging camp. It was such a heartwarming story. When it was over, we were all in tears. Dinner was ready, but none of us felt like eating.

I don't remember many family dinners, but this one will always stand out in my mind and heart; we were all a little closer that day.

This young boy was an incredible example to me. That Thanksgiving, I pledged to accept my trials and do the best I could to live through them. I swore not to whine about what I didn't have, but be grateful for what I did. If I found myself sometimes having a pity party, I told myself to snap out of it. Things could be worse.

* * *

Barbara was one of my mom's best friends and the main reason we moved. She lived above Alotta's and worked as a bartender at the Corral, a local bar that Mom used to go to regularly.

Barbara was a big, buxom blonde. She was tough; she had a reputation of beating up Marines if they misbehaved while she was working. Rumor had it that she would physically kick them out of the bar. It was called being "86ed." If you were 86ed from a bar, you could never go back. I remember hearing that phrase a lot because both Mom and Dad were 86ed from a lot of different establishments. As I've said before, they were mean when they drank.

Barbara had a fifteen-year-old son named Stanley. He was a nice kid, but my sisters and I never hung out with him. Stanley grew marijuana plants on the roof of the apartments. And although we all knew, none of us ever said a word to anyone. One day, someone told Barbara that Stanley was spending a lot of time on the roof. How she managed to get up there was beyond me, since it was dangerous and not easily accessible. She found the plants and took them to the police station; when she got there, she was almost arrested for possession. She was really mad when she got home and immediately came over to our apartment, wanting to know why I hadn't told her that her son was growing marijuana.

I was just getting ready to leave; my boyfriend Dennis was there to pick me up for the movies. Dennis was a little older than I was, already out of school, and considered tough in his own right. Barbara was so furious that she started cussing and accusing me of hiding the fact that Stanley was growing marijuana. I tried to explain that I didn't want to be the one to tell on Stanley, but she was relentless. Dennis didn't like the way Barbara was talking to me and said so. Barbara turned on poor Dennis and pushed him down the flight of stairs that led up to our apartment. Dennis went flying; he crashed at the bottom and stayed there. He was only knocked out for a few seconds, but it was bad. He was pretty banged up, but luckily he didn't break any bones. Barbara went storming back into her own apartment and slammed the door. Barbara really liked me, and she felt that I'd betrayed her by keeping her son's secret.

We tried to find Stanley before he came home, but we didn't know where he was. When he finally walked in, Barbara was waiting for him. She beat the crap out of him, broke his arm, and messed him up pretty bad. I felt sorry for him. She was twice his size and meaner than anyone I'd ever met.

* * *

I thought all of Mom's friends were loud and crazy. Tony Murphy was another friend of Mom's. She was a large woman, but she was very active. She had a fun personality and was always the one laughing and talking loudly. I remember her having a tattoo on each one of her breasts—one said "Sweet" and the other said "Sour." Tony also had three teenage sons who were close to our ages. One day, Mom told us that Tony went to the doctor because she was having pains in her stomach. She had been pregnant for nine months and hadn't even known it; none of us had. She was in her forties when she gave birth to an eight-pound baby girl.

When Mom and her friends would get together, they would pick up sailors and bring them home. If Mom brought them to our apartment, my sisters and I were locked out. We would come home from school or from a friend's house, and the doors would be locked. We could hear music and voices inside, but we knew we needed to go somewhere else.

Sometimes we just sat outside the door because we had no place to go. If we had friends with us, we prayed that the door wouldn't open. Lynn had walked in with a friend one time when Mom had forgotten to lock the door. Lynn said that Mom and all her friends were walking around half-naked. Lynn was so embarrassed, and her friend never came over again.

How do you explain to your friends that your mother is a slut? The word sounds harsh, but it's accurate. We were teenagers and knew that this was not normal behavior for adults.

* * *

My second and final trip to Hillcrest Receiving Home happened the summer before my senior year in high school. Lynn had just gotten married a couple of weeks earlier, and she and Randy had a place of their own.

Mom was experiencing one of her "feel sorry for me" phases. Linda, a thirteen-year-old with a rebellious streak, was giving her problems. If Mom said it was white, Linda would insist it was black.

School had just ended for the summer, and I asked Mom if I could go with a friend to the unemployment office to look for a job. She said I could, but said no when Linda asked to go as well. She needed Linda to walk to the local market to pick up a bag of potatoes. Instead, Linda got mad and ran away from home.

When I returned from the unemployment office, Mrs. Langley, our caseworker, was at the house. Mom was telling her she couldn't take it any longer; she was tired, and Linda was driving her crazy. Mrs. Langley was there to take us to Hillcrest Receiving Home.

What did this mean? What about me? I didn't do anything wrong. This was my summer. I was turning seventeen in a few weeks. I wanted to get a job, go to the beach, and have a great summer. *This was not happening!*

Linda came home, and we were both taken to Hillcrest. It was a Friday night; summer was here, but there was nothing I could do.

It had been six years since we were at Hillcrest. Not much had changed. Our bedrooms were the same; each contained a twin bed covered with a light pink Chenille bedspread, a small dresser, and a nightstand. Every morning we had a bed check. Our beds had to be made perfectly and our rooms had to be clean.

A counselor came in to tell us they had year-round school at Hillcrest. *Great!* I thought things couldn't get any worse until she informed me that there were no kids my age, and I was actually years older than most. After the counselor left, I cried like a baby. I was being punished for my mother's weakness and my little sister's adolescent behavior. After half an hour, I decided that I couldn't do a thing about it; I had better just accept the fact that I was stuck and try to make the best out of a bad situation.

When I wasn't in school, I worked in the nursery. There were always babies that needed love and attention. Once, a baby was brought in that had been found in a trashcan. I spent a lot of time with that little boy; he was so small and beautiful. I couldn't understand how someone could leave a helpless, innocent child that way. He was still at Hillcrest when I left, and I never knew what happened to him.

I also volunteered to work in the kitchen; there were a lot of people to feed. In addition to all the kids, the staff always ate with us too. The food was so good, and there was always enough.

Hillcrest believed in the rewards program. If you worked, you received recognition. The reward was a trip to the San Diego Zoo. Although I grew up in San Diego, I had never been to the zoo. You'd think I would have jumped at the chance to go, but I was seventeen years old. I was torn between the child in me that really wanted to go to the zoo and the teenager that didn't want to be seen with a group of kids who looked like they lived in an orphanage.

The year was 1970, and hip-huggers, tie-dye, peace signs, and long braids were the fashion. The clothes we wore at Hillcrest, however, were more like school uniforms. I wore a crisp white blouse, Capri blue jeans, and Keds with socks. To top it off, on outside trips, we were required to carry a sack lunch.

In the end, my child-self won, and I went to the zoo. There were six of us in total; we all rode in a large blue station wagon. It took me some time to shake the embarrassment of the situation. Once I got past it, I had a great time. I remember being in awe of everything. I still remember the seal show, the damp air and the smell of fish, the giraffes with their long necks and friendly faces, the tropical forests with the exotic birds, and the different kinds of plant life I never even knew existed. The elephants were my favorite. There was a baby elephant that stood right under his mother's tail; I couldn't believe that little thing would eventually be as big as his mother. It was a really great day.

Linda and I spent the entire three months of summer at Hillcrest. The last week before school started, we went to court. I chose to go home with my mom and finish my senior year. Linda chose to live with my older sister Arlene.

CHAPTER 10

Moving On

It was 1970. I was seventeen years old and the only one of my sisters still living at home. My best friend Susan and I were getting ready to go to a party. Susan and I did everything together; she was the one friend that seemed to understand my family's dynamics and didn't judge me for my mother's actions. We were just about to leave when my mom decided to pull her power play by saying, "You can't go anywhere unless you make me a sandwich."

Normally, I wouldn't have cared. I would have just made the sandwich, since it always seemed easier to do what she said instead of arguing or rebelling against her. I was smart enough to know that she definitely had all the power, so why fight it? But tonight was a little different. I didn't think she was even hungry; she just wanted to make a statement. I made her the sandwich, put it on a plate. When I went to hand it to her, I bowed and asked, "Will there be anything else, your highness?"

That really pissed her off because before I knew what hit me, she did. She slapped me right across the face and said in her stern don't-argue-with-me tone, "You're not going anywhere young lady! Go to your room!"

I'm not sure who was more surprised, Mom or me. Poor Susan didn't know what to do. We both went to my room and sat there for a while. I really wanted to go to the party, but I was sure I was grounded. Susan told me to go apologize and maybe she would show some mercy. I didn't think there was a chance, but I didn't have anything to lose. I went in, sat down, and said, "I'm sorry for what I said. I didn't mean it."

Believe it or not, she let me go. I still think I surprised her because I had never talked back or disagreed before. I was always "the good girl." To sass her now was totally out of character.

I learned to keep my mouth shut from then on. Susan was pretty proud of me and we talked about the incident a lot. "Remember when you bowed and called your mom 'your highness'? That was awesome," she'd say to me out of the blue, and we'd just laugh.

My mom was someone to be afraid of. She was one tough lady. Even the boys we dated were afraid of her. It wasn't that she was a big woman, but her presence was big. I think of it now, and I'm still in awe of the power she had over us. I'm not saying it was a good thing. For some reason, she felt she needed that power—that she needed us to fear her. She needed the control. I don't think she had it anywhere else. She knew we were young children, impressionable and easy to manipulate. And boy, did she use her power on us.

As we approached our teens, we started to rebel. My older sisters rebelled in their early teens. Linda was a rebel even before she turned ten. I finally started to say "enough is enough" by the time I was seventeen. It wasn't that I wanted special privileges; I just wanted the meanness to stop. I was tired of being afraid of her. I moved out right after high school graduation, just a few months before my eighteenth birthday.

* * *

When I was seventeen, I went on my first and last blind date.

He picked me up and took me to his apartment, which was also a first for me; he said he needed to pick up his jacket. I didn't know it, but he had already been drinking. I don't know how many beers he had, but when we got to his apartment, he invited me in. I didn't feel any red flags go up because I was naïve, and he was a friend of a friend that I trusted. But I didn't know this guy at all. He could have been Jack the Ripper for all I knew. I went into this stranger's apartment with very little coaxing on his end. What was wrong with me?

His apartment was a good-sized studio with a large, round bed in the middle of the room. I don't remember any other furniture except the refrigerator where the alcohol was. He offered me a beer, which I didn't really want. But I didn't want him to think I was immature, so I took it and just sipped it. He guzzled his and then had another. I thought maybe he was just nervous because of the way he acted. He didn't know what to say, and he seemed a little jittery. He invited me to sit on his round bed, which he thought was the greatest thing ever. Since there was no other place to sit, I sat down. He drank another beer rather quickly, and then he started getting a little touchy-feely. I then realized that because I agreed to come into his apartment, he just assumed everything was fair game. He tried to kiss me, which was disgusting; he was now slurring his words and acting ridiculously.

It was time to leave. I wanted to get out of there and go home. This was not what I had imagined for my first blind date. We were supposed to go to a movie and get something to eat.

"I need to get home," I calmly told him.

His eyes were starting to cross, his speech was slurry, and he was getting silly. If I hadn't been worried about not getting home in time to meet Mom's curfew, I probably would have realized that this guy was just young and stupid; he'd gotten nervous about our blind date and had drank too much.

We left his apartment, and I saw that he was staggering. He wasn't going to be able to drive. I didn't have my license yet, but I knew how to drive.

"Give me the keys," I demanded, and he didn't hesitate.

He was bombed. I opened the car door and then reached over to open the passenger side to let him in. *I should just leave him here*, I thought. Then I looked around for a minute and realized his car had a stick shift.

"You have to help me," I said as he got inside. "I've never driven a stick before."

Before he nodded off, he told me how to push in the clutch, put it into gear, and then ease back up on it. What should have taken half an hour to drive to my house took hours. I found myself going in circles around the block to avoid having to stop and put the car in gear. I hadn't gotten used to the clutch; I would let up on it, and the car would stall. My date drifted in and out of consciousness. When he would open his eyes, he'd grin and tell me I was so pretty, and then he'd try to touch me. I was trying so hard to concentrate on driving a stick; having to fend off his advances just made me madder and madder.

I finally pulled into the parking lot of our apartment. I just parked, put on the brake, and left him there passed out. I was late getting home and thought for sure I was in trouble. When I walked in, Mom was in the kitchen. She saw the look on my face and asked, "What happened?"

I proceeded to tell her that I had left my date in the car. She said, "You can't just leave him down there, he'll freeze."

I was still so mad; I told her I didn't care what happened to him because I hated him. She told me, "Mary, take him a blanket at least."

She looked genuinely worried. I said that I had no intention of going near him, and I went to bed.

Mom took him a blanket and a pillow, and the next morning she invited him for coffee. You'd think she would be mad at this guy, a perfect stranger who put her daughter in harm's way. But, instead, she felt sorry for him and treated him like an old friend. She never ceased to amaze me. In fact, he did turn out to be a nice guy. He wasn't boyfriend material, but he was a nice person. We continued to be friends for years, but we never went out on a date again.

* * *

I was a senior now, soon to be out on my own—off to college and starting a new life. I knew I was going to be moving out as soon as I graduated from high school. That was a given. The only thing now was how to spend my last year in high school. This was my second year at the same school, so I had some friends from the previous year and some from the two junior high schools I had gone to. I knew one thing for sure: I didn't want to be that same, shy girl who was too afraid of making mistakes or saying the wrong things to really enjoy herself.

It's hard being a kid, and if people tell you something different, they are lying to you. I wanted to fit in so badly that I first tried acting like I was all that. I thought the cool kids were into partying; I wanted them to think I was worldly and experienced, when in reality I had just spent my entire summer in Hillcrest. My mom didn't allow us much freedom, so my life experiences were limited.

I was in my homeroom class when one of the popular kids asked someone across the desk from me if she was going to Paula's party on Saturday night. I knew Paula, and I knew about the party, so I acted like I was going. I said, "I'm going to Paula's."

I was sure my mom wouldn't let me go, but I acted like I went out all the time. Who was I kidding? They knew I was lying; they had never seen me at a party before. Who did I think I was to include myself in their conversation? They didn't say anything, and sometimes a look is worse than words. Both girls just stared at me as if to say, "Mind your own business. Who was talking to you, anyway?"

I felt like an idiot, and if I could have left right then and there, I would have. But I just turned around and acted like nothing happened.

I ended up hanging around the same group of friends I had met the year before and having a great senior year. Sometimes you have to just accept the way things are. I was hoping to change my life by changing my friends, but that's not the way it works. Sometimes, the people you think you want as your friends end up being the people you have nothing in common with. I had already made friends with people I had something in common with—people that liked me for me, just the way I was. Those people are still my friends today.

* * *

The hall monitor came into our homeroom class, but I wasn't paying attention. I had never been called out of class for anything, so when the teacher called my name, I was shocked. When he motioned for me to come to the front of the class, I sat there thinking I hadn't heard him correctly. I closed my book, got up, and slowly walked to his desk. He handed me the call slip to the office. I couldn't think of what it could be. Maybe Mom was sick or something had happened to one of my sisters. Other than that, I couldn't imagine. I walked into the office, gave the lady behind the counter the call slip, and was told to sit down and wait for them to call me. I sat down and honestly couldn't think of what they would want with me at the office. I hadn't done anything wrong, so I wasn't worried.

The lady behind the counter called my name. As I stood up, she pointed to the principal's office. I had never even talked to the principal before. What could it be? The principal was behind his desk, and he motioned for me to sit down. The door was closed behind me. He started the conversation with a question: "Marianne, do you remember getting a citation this past summer for driving without a license?"

I just stared at him. I was speechless. Of course I remembered getting that citation, but the question in my head was, *How do YOU know I got a citation?*

"The San Diego Police Department called the school looking for you," he went on to explain. "They want you to report to court next week with your mother."

All I heard was "with your mother." I took down all the information—the date, the time, and where we were supposed to go—and went back to class, but the day was a total loss. How was I going to tell my mother that I took her car while she was in the hospital having an operation, and that I got stopped by the police because the car was smoking? I was seventeen years old and did not have my license.

A boy I knew and had a crush on asked me to give him a ride to El Cajon. I knew I wasn't supposed to drive, and I also knew my mom would kill me if she found out. He convinced me that it would be okay, saying that he would drive there and I would drive back.

When I was driving back, the highway patrol pulled me over for excessive smoke. When he asked for my license, I played dumb and pretended to look for my purse. I told him I must have accidentally left it at home. He wrote me a ticket for the excessive smoke but also for driving without my license. He was really nice. The incident happened before we went to Hillcrest. I meant to tell Mom, but then everything happened with Linda and Hillcrest, and I never got around to it. I was hoping the police would forget all about it, but obviously that didn't happen. Now I needed to fess up and take the punishment. I would rather face the police again than have to face my mom. Mom was so unpredictable; she would lose control over something mild and be totally calm during something major. We were always unsure how she would react.

Mom was spending most days (and nights) drinking down at Alotta's, so it was difficult to find the right time to talk to her. I didn't have much time; we needed to report to the juvenile court in just a few days.

When I got home, the house was empty. I knew where she was, but I couldn't decide whether now was a good time or not. I decided to just do it. I went downstairs and peeked in the door of Alotta's. It was always so dark at first, and I hated it because I knew the people in the bar could see me, but I couldn't see a thing. I stood there while my eyes adjusted to the dark and then stepped further in. I knew exactly where she was sitting because the regulars at Alotta's always sat in the same spot. She was sitting with her friends, and they were all in a good mood. Mom was smiling; someone must have said something funny because several of the other people were laughing. I walked up to the bar and tapped Mom on the shoulder. When she turned, she seemed genuinely happy to see me. This was a good sign. She ordered me a Coke and re-introduced me to all her friends.

After the Coke was served, I took a drink to calm my nerves and then said, "Mom, I need to tell you something."

She asked, "What's up?"

"Remember when you went in the hospital for your hernia operation?"

She said, "I remember. What's going on?"

I then confessed the whole thing. I told her that a friend (because he was a friend) really needed a ride to El Cajon, that I had taken her car without her permission, and I had gotten a ticket for excessive smoke and not having a driver's license. I told her that they tracked me down at school and that we needed to go to court next week. I said it really fast without taking a breath. I felt safe being in Alotta's, and I was banking on her not yelling at me in front of her friends. But again, she was so unpredictable. Who knew? She didn't say anything for a few minutes, and then she asked when and where we needed to go. I told her all the details, and she patted my hand and said, "Okay."

I knew I looked as shocked as I felt, sitting there waiting for something else, something worse. But nothing happened. She said okay, and that was it.

We went to court the following week. It turned out to be really painless. The police officer who gave me the ticket didn't show up, but he left a note with the ticket saying that I was a sweet girl, very polite, who seemed responsible. The judge gave me a lecture about driving without a license and that was that. All was dismissed.

The anticipation of not knowing what Mom was going to do was more punishment than anything I could have imagined. How did she do that? She had us so deathly afraid of her that I would rather have gone to jail than face her. I'm not sure if that is good parenting or child abuse.

* * *

Dean was one of the nicest guys I had ever met. We graduated from high school together. Everyone liked Dean. He always had a smile on his face and a twinkle in his eyes. In high school he was a surfer; he spent all his extra time at the beach, waiting for the perfect wave. I remember going with him and all his friends to watch surfing movies at all the local high schools. I was a terrible swimmer myself, not strong enough to fight the currents. After having to be rescued by various lifeguards, I stayed on the shore and became a spectator of surfing. I spent many afternoons or Saturdays just watching Dean surf.

Dean had a dream; he was going to make surfboards. He had it all planned out. He was going to live in Hawaii, surf, and make boards. I really believed he could do it.

His girlfriend all through high school was Paulette. We were actually friends for a while. She was a year younger than us, and we went to few dances together. She was crazy about him.

Dean was the kind of person that never judged anyone. He knew I lived above Alotta's, but he never treated me differently than he treated anyone else. We were friends, and I loved him for the person he was.

One summer he and Paulette were having problems, so Dean and I hung out a lot. We never hung out as boyfriend and girlfriend but as good friends. I went with him to the beach or to watch a movie with his friends. We enrolled at Southwestern College together, and he would give me a ride every once in a while.

Paulette didn't like that. She thought we were more than friends and decided she didn't like me anymore. She told Dean's mom some pretty awful things about me and used the fact that I lived above Alotta's as proof positive—anyone who lived there *had* to be bad. I had never met Dean's mom, so when I heard that she didn't want him hanging out with someone like me, my feelings were badly hurt. I was condemned for my mother's choice of residence.

Dean and I remained friends. Paulette got pregnant, and they were married right after that summer. Dean never made surfboards. He ended up joining the National City Police Department.

I had an office in National City for years. One day I had a break-in. When I got to the office, I found Dean's business card. I couldn't believe it was the same person I knew in school. I called him immediately and left a message. He came by to say hello. It had been years, and Dean looked almost the same except the twinkle in his eye was gone; he had a tough time on the force. He was hospitalized because a suspect on ecstasy went crazy and really beat him up, and he eventually retired from the force. He was still married to Paulette and had three daughters. It was good to see him after all those years. I'd like to say that he looked happy, but something was missing. He didn't have the same smile I remembered.

* * *

After high school, I enrolled at Southwestern Junior College. While I was at Hillcrest, I decided I needed to go to college. I wanted to become a juvenile probation officer to help the children from Hillcrest and others like them—children with difficult home lives. I knew how frightening it was to go to a strange place and live with strangers, and I wanted to help them understand that they had options. At Hillcrest, I had seen many kids choosing to go home to abuse and neglect rather than face the unknown.

I loved all the sociology, psychology, and law enforcement classes associated with juvenile law, and I got a job working on campus. It was great because the college worked around my schedule. I first worked at the counseling center and then in the book loan department. It wasn't easy; I was on my own. Minimum wage was $1.10 per hour, and I had to pay my own rent and food. I remember eating a lot of peanut butter sandwiches, but somehow it all worked out.

During my last semester, I worked with the Chula Vista Police Department on my internship. They assigned me three families to work with. Until then, I hadn't realized how hard the field I had chosen would be. In my fantasy, I had envisioned helping all these needy children, counseling them to stay in school, rescuing them from abusive parents, and doing all the great things I had seen on television. But that wasn't the way it was. The probation officer's job was to oversee the families and to help them cope with everyday life. These families had real problems, real life issues. I worked with one family from New York that had to move out-of-state to escape an abusive father. The man had already been in jail for setting fire to their house while they slept. One of the children, a three-year-old boy, was severely burned; he lost sight in one eye and had burns on sixty percent of his body. His seven-year-old sister did not have full use of her hands and arms because the skin had fused together. After several surgeries, she was still in pain. The older brother suffered a head injury from the father's previous abuse.

I had a hard time with this case; I think it hit too close to home. I found myself having nightmares regularly, imagining that the father was coming after me. I would run and hide, but he would always find me. After working on my internship for a few months, I had a serious talk with my guidance counselor. We agreed that I was too emotionally invested—I wanted to adopt all the children I was hired to oversee. I wore my emotions on my sleeve, and that was not a good thing if I wanted to work in the field. Probation officers needed to think clearly, see things as they truly were, and make wise decisions. I wanted to save all the families and destroy all the bad guys. I was not thinking clearly. I decided to take a break from school for a while, and I moved away from San Diego for a few years just to clear my head. I lived in San Francisco with friends and took a job working for a downtown accounting firm. It was an adventure, and it gave me some time to figure things out—to decide what I wanted to do with the rest of my life.

While working for the accounting firm, I had the opportunity to work on Fisherman's Wharf. We had a client whose office was located on the wharf. Their secretary was sitting at her desk one day and suddenly went blind. It was the strangest thing—she was young, in her twenties. The doctors said she had somehow injured a nerve that controlled her eyesight. My boss volunteered me to watch the office until the client could get a replacement.

Fisherman's Wharf is located on Pier 29 in San Francisco, near Alcatraz Island, the Golden Gate Bridge, and Angel Island. It's on the water's edge, where all the ships cross the bay.

Working on Fisherman's Wharf was like working in the middle of a county fair. There were artists set up on the sidewalks. Street musicians and food vendors were on every corner. I rode BART, the underground transportation, and then took the San Francisco trolley the rest of the way. It was so exciting.

The Vietnam War was ending, and there were protesters everywhere. Young, ex-military men with long hair were hanging out with girls who had no makeup and wore long tie-dyed skirts, fringed jackets, and their hair in braids. Janice Joplin and Jimmy Hendrix had died; it was the tail end of the love movement, but there were still posters everywhere that read "Make Love Not War."

My sister Lynn and her second husband Ron came to visit. I took a couple of days off and showed them San Francisco. We rode a ferry to Alcatraz Island and toured "The Rock," the prison that had housed Al Capone, Machine Gun Kelly, and the birdman of Alcatraz from the 30s to the 60s.

While riding the ferry, the captain had to come up on deck and ask two young men that were passionately kissing and groping each other to please stop. This was 1974, and the gay movement was starting to find its footing. We were a little shocked and a bit uncomfortable. I was twenty-two years old, and this was the first time I had seen two men kissing.

Later that night, Mom called. I told her about our day and all we had done. I also told her about the couple on the ferry. She didn't seem surprised. She told me there were a lot of different people and that I needed to be more open to the ways of the world. She said that I didn't have to be a part of everything, but I should be more accepting of other people's choices.

I had to think about that for a while. I was starting to realize that I had been sheltered. The world was changing, and I had no idea how much.

* * *

Back in 1965, when I was thirteen years old, the first episode of "The Monkeys" was broadcast on NBC, and *The Sound of Music* won five Academy Awards.

For my birthday that year, Lynn bought me a training bra that I didn't really need. She either felt sorry for me or was making fun of me; either way, I was so embarrassed when I opened the package in front of her boyfriend.

I started to babysit a little boy named Jimbo that year. I loved babies and babysat as often as I could to earn money and to get out of the house. My best friend at that time was Debbie; she was two years older and had introduced me to Linda, Jimbo's mom. Jimbo had blond hair, blue eyes, and was truly adorable. Linda was divorced and lived with her mother, and I babysat a lot for her. I actually stayed a whole summer with them, and it was one of my best. As long as I gave Mom my babysitting money, she had no problem with me being gone.

Linda had a sister who married her high school sweetheart, Gary. Debbie knew Gary's younger brother, Jerry, from high school. Jerry and his best friend started coming over when I babysat, and Debbie and I both had the biggest crush on Jerry. I never told anyone about my crush because Debbie was my best friend. She was older, and I was just a kid. I was sure he didn't even know I existed.

One Friday night I was babysitting by myself. Jerry came over, and he told me he knew I liked him. (I guess my gawking at him like an idiot gave me away.) I was sitting at the kitchen table when he leaned down and lightly kissed me on the lips. He wanted to see what I would do, and of course I did the most mature thing I could think of. I panicked. I got up, went to Jimbo's room, picked up the sleeping baby (along with his blanket and pillow), and proceeded to lock myself in the bathroom.

I stayed there until Jerry left. I was scared and intrigued at the same time. When I was sure he was gone, I came out, put the baby back to bed, and that was it. I never told anyone. I wasn't sure it had really happened, and if it did, I wasn't sure what it meant. Was he teasing me or did he kiss me for real? I thought about Jerry a lot, and I wrote his name over and over again (that's what girls did). He was my first kiss, and I knew I would love him forever.

A few weeks later, Jerry's other brother, Ronnie, was killed on a motorcycle. Debbie and I walked to the funeral; his brother was really popular and there were so many kids from school there. The school had announced that anyone leaving school to attend the funeral would be suspended. I wondered how they could suspend that many kids. Jerry stood off to the side by himself, looking sad and alone.

I didn't talk to Jerry again for thirteen years. I had seen him on the street, or in his car, but he never came over again. Linda and Jimbo moved out of state. I went back home, finished school, went to college, and moved to Fontana, California. All three of my sisters had relocated there and we always stayed close.

My parents still lived in San Diego. On occasion, my sisters and I would drive down and visit my mom; sometimes we would go dancing or just hang out with friends. One of my high school friends, Lupe, worked as a waitress at a local nightclub. She dated one of the guys in the band, and it was always fun to go there because we knew most of the people.

One Friday night a group of us went dancing. Lupe came up to me after we were seated and asked me if I remembered Jerry Hill. I told her, "Are you kidding? He was my first kiss!"

She said he was sitting at the bar. She had asked him if he remembered me, and he said the only Marys he knew were his mother's best friend and a little girl that used to babysit. He came over and joined our table. We danced and talked about old times; he gave me a business card and told me to call him, but I never did.

Two months later we drove down to San Diego again to see Lupe. I asked her if she had seen Jerry, and she said he hadn't been in since the last time I was down. About an hour later, Lupe came over and said, "You'll never guess who just walked in."

I walked over to the bar and there he was, paying for a beer and getting ready to play some pool. I tapped him on the shoulder, and he turned and looked at me. The look on his face was one of surprise and joy, which made me feel good. He told me later, "When I turned around to see who tapped me on the shoulder, all I saw were your beautiful, green eyes and the biggest, sweetest smile. I knew right there that you were the one."

We talked all night, and we spent the next day together and the next. When I went home this time, we promised to write, and we did.

I quit my job and moved back to my mother's house in May 1979. Jerry and I were engaged in July and married in November that same year. We had our first of four sons four years later. After thirty-plus years, we are still happily married. Life is so unpredictable—so full of surprises.

Was it destiny that I visited Lupe the first time Jerry ever went to that club? Was it destiny that neither of us went back there until that very same night, two months later?

I like to think these things don't happen by themselves. I like to think we all have guardian angels. Jerry thinks his brother Ronnie had a hand in our reuniting. It doesn't matter who or what put us together; it just matters that it happened.

CHAPTER 11

Memories of Mom

When I first started writing this book, memories of my mom kept coming back in bits and pieces. At first all the bad memories surfaced. All I could recall were the times I felt terrible or awful things happened. As time went by, I started to remember more than just the bad things. Of course, there was so much more to Mom than her faults.

As I go day to day, living my life, I think of qualities I have, good or bad. Then I think about my mom. Did she do this? Did she say that? Did she teach me this? Did I learn that from her?

Last night I had a nail appointment with Tiffany, whom I truly adore. She is about thirty years old, and she moved to the United States from Vietnam. In the two years I've been going to Tiffany, I have seen her grow. She was so shy at first and she hardly talked at all. But now she talks all the time, sticks up for herself, and has definitely become Americanized. It's cute because a hair/nail salon is a gossip capital. She filled me in on all the gossip that happened in the four weeks since I was last in. One thing she said was that "ladies live to gossip." This statement got me thinking. I know I do my share of gossiping. I try not to bad-talk others, but I do repeat things I probably shouldn't.

So I asked myself, did Mom teach me to gossip? As I thought about this question, I honestly tried to recap events and conversations I had with my mom or things I'd overheard her say. I could not remember one time that I heard her gossiping. I do remember she used to always say, "If you can't say something nice, don't say anything at all," but I couldn't remember her talking about anyone or repeating other people's business.

Mom was pretty outspoken. If she had a beef with someone, she just went face-to-face with that person. I think Mom's philosophy was, "I have enough problems of my own. I have no time or room to talk about anyone else's."

Another quality I liked about my mom was that she never taught us to be prejudiced. Everyone was the same in her eyes. She had a variety of friends of all races, religions, and creeds. What people did in their own homes was their business; she was never judgmental. She had a lot of homosexual friends. As long as they did not hurt another human being, what they did was fine with her. She would say, "You never know what life is going to hand you. We must never say never."

What I'm learning in my search for self is that yes, my mom had her faults. In my memory bank, her bad qualities overshadowed her good. But it's important that I remember she did have some amazing qualities.

When my life is finished and I have left many memories (good or bad) behind, I hope my loved ones remember the good I have done. I know I have made my share of mistakes. We are all human; we are expected to make mistakes. What's important is what we do about the mistakes we make.

It's not until you've lived your life do you realize how fragile it is. As a child you think you are never going to die, you have your ups and downs and you get your bumps and bruises. Some of us get more bruises than others, but somehow we live through it. Just like my paper dolls—a little tape and they can last forever.

* * *

I believe each life will be judged by those we leave behind. What we do will be remembered by someone. Make your mark. Be the best person you can be, so in the end you will be remembered for the good things you've done. Then any mistakes you make will be overshadowed by the good that you do.

CHAPTER 12

Mom Gets Sick

One night we received a phone call from the San Diego Police Department. Mom was leaving her favorite bar when she put the car in drive (instead of reverse) and ran straight into a residential house. She was taken to the hospital for observation, and then we took her home. This happened in 1996 when Mom was seventy-five years old, and it was a wake-up call to us. She was getting sick. The house Mom ran into was the home of a lady that was turning one hundred years old that same week. Mom was devastated; from that moment on she never had another drink. Although she continued to visit all the same bars she frequented before, she now drank only cranberry juice and visited with her friends.

Hindsight taught us that we should have taken her keys from her or at least questioned whether she should still drive. We had assumed her actions were because she was drinking, and now that she was no longer drinking, we assumed she would be fine. Little did we know that Mom was going downhill.

Mom was on her way to my house one afternoon when she had car trouble. She was able to get her car pushed into a bank's empty parking lot where several good Samaritans stopped to help her. They were able to get her car started, and Mom got into the driver's seat while another woman stood inside the open car door to make sure she could start the engine by herself. When the engine started, Mom immediately put the car in reverse and stepped on the gas. The car door slammed into the woman standing there, throwing her into the air. Mom's car proceeded to hit the woman's car and then stopped when it struck a tree. (However, the tree snapped and fell onto a bus that was waiting at its stop.) The poor woman was hospitalized with broken ribs and a punctured lung. Fortunately, no one else was hurt, but the woman who helped my mom had to stay in the hospital for several weeks and was never the same. We felt terrible. We had no idea that Mom was starting to get so confused or that she was on the brink of dementia.

From that moment on, Mom was no longer able to drive. She still lived on her own, but that only lasted another couple of months. She started acting irrationally, making phones calls to the police at all hours of the night. Once she called and said she could not identify a suitcase that was in her living room. The police were called, and in turn they called me. The suitcase belonged to her granddaughter who had spent the night with her and accidentally left it behind.

She started calling our house at all hours, asking what time it was, getting her days and nights mixed up. My husband Jerry had the phone on his side of the bed and he was so patient with her. He would tell her to look out her window; if it was dark, then she should go back to bed. Another time we received a call from the manager of her apartment telling us that she was roaming around with no clothes on. We picked her up and brought her to our house.

We decided it was time to move Mom into a care center. We tried an assisted living center, but after only one month an attendant called and said she needed more care than they could offer. They suggested we move her to a board and care where she would get more one-on-one attention. We tried several different homes, but each one was a thirty-minute drive, which made it hard to see her often.

We had a board and care home located on our block, only two houses down from ours, so we put our name on the waiting list. As soon as they had an opening, we grabbed it. Now we could pick her up daily and bring her to our house to visit. We would return her at night, where she would have round-the-clock care. I could still go to work during the day and visit with her in the evening. It was the perfect situation.

I would either bring her down to the house or have one of my boys bring her down in her wheelchair. I had a bed set up in the family room so she could relax and watch TV. I would comb her hair, or put lotion on her feet and hands, or just sit with her and watch TV. I wasn't sure she knew I was there, but I felt comforted. There were times she didn't seem to be fully aware of where she was or who we were. That was heartbreaking, but then there were times when she seemed to know us, and we would have a nice visit. Eventually, she hardly recognized any of us.

One day I was dropping my youngest son off at school, and on the way back I heard (and then saw) an ambulance turn on to my street. I knew immediately it was for my mom. I followed the ambulance down the street, parked, and was in the board and care before the ambulance even got there. Mom was in her bed, and she looked funny. Her body was stiff and in a strange position. Her caregiver said that when she went to wake her for breakfast, Mom was lying like that, unresponsive. The caregiver had immediately called 911.

The paramedics took her vitals and then loaded her into the ambulance to take her to the hospital. I followed behind and waited as they admitted her to the emergency room. The doctor said he wasn't sure what the situation was, but if there was family I wanted to call, I should do it because this could very well be it.

I immediately called my husband and then my sisters. My oldest sister Arlene lived a couple of hours away. I hated calling her when I didn't know what was really happening, but she agreed to come. She and her husband Dyke drove down. We all sat in the waiting room.

The doctor finally told us that Mom's meds needed to be adjusted, and once they adjusted them, she would be better.

But Mom continued to get worse. She got pneumonia and ended up back in the hospital. One morning a nurse called me and said that I should come to the hospital immediately. She said my mom was slipping away.

* * *

I've been sitting in my car for several hours. I still have to call my sisters and let them know that Mom is gone.

I'm not ready to do that yet, so I'll just sit here in my car. It's a 1996 Rodeo; I had it washed yesterday, and it smells clean. The windows are down, it's early in the morning, and I can hear the birds chirping and see the dew on the grass. These are gentle reminders that life still goes on.

But I still don't understand. *How will I live without her?*

Epilogue

Toy Soldiers

I'm startled when my cell phone rings. I reach for the phone sitting in my lap. I'm still in my car, and I guess I've been sitting here for some time. "Hello?" I say. It's my sixteen-year-old son, Timothy.

"Hi Mom," he says. "Are you alright? Dad called and told us that Grandma passed away. I'm so sorry."

I hesitate to answer because I'm too choked up to speak. Just the sound of his voice brings me to tears. I love him so much—I love all my boys so much.

* * *

"Lets go to the woods, Mommy. Can we go to the woods?" Timmy pleaded with me as we pulled away from the curb at Grandma's house.

It had been a really long day at work, and I was exhausted. But looking at those four eager faces—eight-year-old Jeremy, six-year-old Timothy, five-year-old Jonathan, and one-year-old Preston—how could I say no?

"Of course we can go to the woods, but just for a little while. Mommy needs to get dinner started."

Their little heads bobbed up and down in agreement, and off we went. It was only a short distance from Grandma's house and on the way home, so it wasn't too great of an effort on my part. The closer we got to the woods, the more excited the boys got. They giggled and squealed as we turned down the winding road. The trees were high, and some hung over into the road. The sun peeked between the branches as we drove. At times the shaded trees were so thick that it felt like nighttime, until we emerged to see the sun still blazing in the sky. The ride went over hills and valleys, and the boys held their tummies and giggled as we went up and then down again.

The ride through the woods lasted about two minutes, and the boys were completely sedated and happy. I turned around and headed for home.

"The woods" was actually just a tree-lined street. There was no forest, just a tree-lined street. We still drive down that street almost twenty years later, and it's still the woods to all of us.

* * *

Parenting is not easy—it's always a work in progress—but I'm striving to do the best that I can. I've learned that it takes so little effort to bring joy into someone's life. My hope is simply this: that these four little boys will have good memories forever.

(from left to right) Tim, 10; Jeremy, 12; Preston, 4; Jonathan, 9.

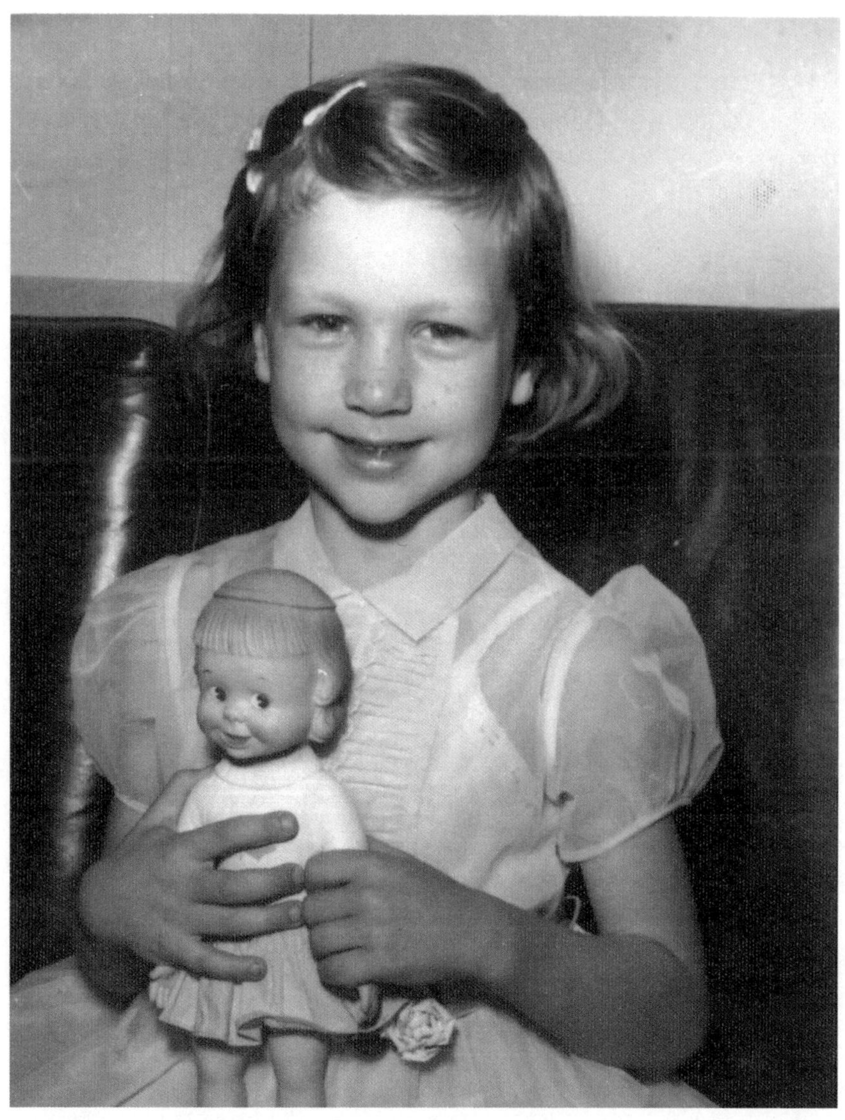

Marianne Joseph Hill, age 5 (The doll was a prop from the photographer.)